敲開你的心扉

Open Your Mind

by Sheng-yen Lu

A US Daden Culture Publication

US Daden Culture LLC
3440 Foothill Blvd.
Oakland, CA 94601
U.S.A.
Website: www.usdaden.com
Email: us.daden.culture@gmail.com

Lu, Sheng-yen, 1945-
Open Your Mind/by Sheng-yen Lu;
translated by Monita Chan;
edited by Janet Ho and Kai Chung Ho;
proofread by Jessie Loh.

Library of Congress Control Number (PCN): 2017942163
ISBN-13: 978-0-9963807-4-4
ISBN-10: 0-9963807-4-4
1. True Buddha School. 2. Chinese-Tibetan Buddhism.
Cover design and layout by US Daden Culture Design Team
Photograph by US Daden Culture
Set in Minion Pro 12
US Daden books are printed on acid-free paper and meet the guidelines for the permanence and durability set by the Council of Library Resources.

Printed in the U.S.A.

$12.00
ISBN 978-0-9963807-4-4
51200>
9 780996 380744

Special Acknowledgements

The True Buddha Translation Teams (TBTTs) would like to express the highest honor and deepest gratitude to Living Buddha Lian-sheng Sheng-yen Lu and Master Lianxiang for their continuing support and guidance on the translation effort. Without their compassion, wisdom, blessings, and encouragement, this project would not have reached fruition.

In addition, we would like to acknowledge the diligent work put forth by the following volunteers on this project: the leader of US Daden, Master Lianseng; Monita Chan (translator), Janet Ho and Kai Chung Ho (editors), Jessie Loh (proofreader), and Renee Cordsen (publication). We would like to thank these dedicated and selfless volunteers who have contributed their time and effort to promote the works of Living Buddha Lian-sheng, and to support the publications of US Daden Culture.

We would also like to extend our sincere appreciation to all of the other volunteers who work behind the scenes, facilitating the translation process, and handling administrative responsibilities.

May all volunteers be blessed with immeasurable merits. May all sentient beings benefit from the ocean of wisdom.

Table of Contents

My cultivation is just like my writing, in that it has not ever been interrupted in the past forty years.

Sheng-yen Lu

Preface: Open Your Mind

In October 2011, I had expounded the dharma in both Seattle Ling Shen Ching Tze Temple and Rainbow Temple in the United States for a duration of two months. During these two months, the dharmas that I taught included numerous essential and precious pith instructions.

In addition:

At the "Chang Hong Temple" of Panama, I expounded the mnemonic of the "Nine-Syllable Mantra Syllable-Cutting Formula" and "Kalachakra's Sun-Moon Disc Practice," which were very hard to come by.

At the "St. Dak Temple" in the state of Florida of the United States, I transmitted the secret among secrets, the "Supreme Divine Water Practice."

At the "Lian Sheng Temple" in the city of Philadelphia of the United States, I taught "The Padmakumara Dharma Lineage Flow," which was deeply unfathomable.

At the "True Buddha Diamond Temple of New York" in the United States, I preached "The Sadhana of Mahapratisara Bodhisattva," which was really rare and precious.

At the “Houston True Buddha Temple” in the state of Texas of the United States, I transmitted “Kalachakra’s Five Wheels” and explained “Nirvana is Joy.” These were hardly heard of in this world.

Etc…

The pith instructions in these teachings and the practice of diligent cultivation originated from my lineage masters to whom I pay homage to:

Reverend Liaoming.

His Holiness the Sixteenth Dharma King (Karmapa).

Vajra Master Sakya Zhengkong.

Vajra Master Thubten Dargye.

And all Masters.

My cultivation is just like my writing, in that it has not ever been interrupted in the past forty years. In fact, in this current life, it is difficult to find anyone with such perseverance and fortitude towards meditative practice. Therefore, my blessing [to sentient beings] is limitless and so is my achievement.

I also predicted:

1. Attainment of Buddhahood in this current life.
2. Rebirth in the pure land.
3. Eternally living in this world and turning the dharma wheel.

In this life, I am a cultivator who has set the foundation in benefiting the generations of cultivators to come. This is my wish and is also the vow that I made.

* **

Over forty years ago, I was at the “Jade Emperor Temple” of Taichung where I coincidentally met “Madame Lin Qiandai” and was guided by her. Golden Mother of the Jade Pond descended and opened my Divine Eyes.

Golden Mother of the Jade Pond said, "I have been looking for you for a long time!"

And said, "I have helped to transfer your [military] posting so that you will be permanently stationed in Taichung." (Referring to my life in the army.)

And said, "A great opportunity will arise and a Great Dharma will be passed on to you."

And said, "Follow the buddhas wholeheartedly, practice wholeheartedly, and perform good deeds wholeheartedly."

(I was twenty-six years old at that time.)

Starting from that day, I encountered miracles almost every day to the extent that I could not finish recounting all of them even if I were to do so.

I flew to the buddha land of Padmasambhava.

I visited ancient tombs or caves.

I was swallowed through the mouth of Padmasambhava, and then reborn from Padmasambhava.

Padmasambhava transformed into rainbow light. I merged into the rainbow light and bathed in all the empowerments from the lineage of Padmasambhava; the flow of his lineage empowerments diffused through my eighty-four thousand pores.

I experienced:

The splitting of the sky.

The shaking of the mountains, rivers, and lands.

I wrote my experiences, but was misconstrued by people as mad.

(Therein lies the secret of the awakening of my faith)

I wish this book, *Open Your Mind,* can make people generate faith in practicing Buddhism.

Living Buddha Lian-sheng Sheng-yen Lu
17102 NE 40th Ct,
Redmond, WA 98052
U.S.A.

1. Am I a Mad Man?

I may look a little crazy, but this craziness is hardly enough for admittance to the mental hospital.

My reasons for "craziness" are:

Being friends with ghosts.

Being friends with gods.

Being friends with bodhisattvas.

Being friends with buddhas.

These reasons may be enough to cause people to classify me as a going-to-be-crazy person, because similar types of people have been locked up in the mental hospital.

There is a joke [about mental patients]:

The Dean of a mental hospital asked a patient, "Who told you that you are Jesus?"

The patient answered, "God."

Another patient who passed by then told the patient who claimed to be Jesus, "I did not tell you that you are Jesus."

After reading this joke, I had a big laugh.

Therefore, when people call me a madman upon knowing my

situation, I cannot blame them because I am not very different from a madman.

I am otherwise a normal person.

When it is time to sleep, I sleep.

When it is time to cultivate, I cultivate.

When it is time to write, I write.

When it is time to paint, I paint.

I do not wear thick underwear in the summer, and I definitely do not wear just a t-shirt in the winter. I put on a scarf when I feel cold, and a thin robe when I feel warm.

I have a normal life.

I neither break laws nor violate precepts, and I lead a disciplined life.

I have breakfast at 6 o'clock in the morning, lunch at noon time, and dinner at 6 o'clock in the evening.

I socialize with people normally.

I said:

I am not a saint, I am not great, I am just an ordinary person. Everything runs naturally, and being natural is the path (the Tao). Laozi said: "Tao follows the laws of nature."

I think:

"Saints must be the most unwise people in the world." (Self-binding)

I understand the philosophy of the "Book of Changes":

"A great man's virtue is in harmony with that of heaven and earth, his brightness is in harmony with that of the sun and the moon, his orderliness is in harmony with those of the four seasons, and his [encounters of] auspiciousness and ominousness are in harmony with those of gods and ghosts."

1. Observe morality.
2. Purify body, speech, and mind.
3. Live naturally.
4. Understand the reasons behind auspiciousness and

ominousness, and bad and good fortune.

The four items listed above are in tandem with the philosophy of the *Book of Changes*. Being friends with gods and ghosts is something which I have in excess of a normal person, and therefore I am a person who is able tell the auspiciousness and ominousness of things.

I have numerous ghost friends, and they are all my good friends.

One year, I was facing an imminent calamity.

A ghost told me, "A big imminent calamity."

I asked, "What to do?"

The ghost answered, "Escape!"

I asked, "How to escape?"

The ghost answered, "Create a diversion."

(Make people think that you are here, when in fact, you are somewhere else, ha ha ha!)

My ghost friends helped me, and my celestial friends also helped me, so that I could breeze through a disaster.

I am not bragging about the friendships that I have with ghosts, gods, bodhisattvas, and buddhas, because anyone can do so. Yao and Shun were human beings, and anyone could be Yao or Shun; Shakyamuni Buddha was a human being, and you could also be Shakyamuni Buddha. On this point, I am not deceiving you!

In fact, there are also ghosts at "True Buddha Quarter," but these ghosts are my disciples who took refuge in me.

Sheng-yen Lu

2. Ghosts Live in My House

I have moved several times while I lived in Seattle in the state of Washington of the United States.

The first time, I moved from "Ballard" to "True Buddha Quarter."

The second time, I moved from "True Buddha Quarter" to "Phantom Lake."

The third time, I moved from "Phantom Lake" to "South Mountain Retreat."

The fourth time, I moved from "South Mountain Retreat" to "New South Mountain Retreat."

There was a ghost at the basement of my Ballard house, and this ghost was not too friendly to Foqing and Foqi.

When I was moving out, I could even hear them sighing in the basement.

"New South Mountain Retreat" is my last home and it occupies two acres of land. It is a bigger house and two ghosts live there.

Every morning when I wake up, I have to walk along a long corridor. When I pass by the guest restroom located along that corridor, a loud "KA" noise would always sound.

The same thing happens everyday.

As it turned out, the ghosts in the restroom were startled by the light emitting from me.

Initially, there was just only one ghost, but later, another ghost surprisingly moved into "New South Mountain Retreat" when I happened to stay in Taiwan longer than usual.

These two ghosts are not harmful to us.

One of the ghosts would even salute me in military style, because he used to be an American soldier and he knew that I was a former Lieutenant commander. Therefore, every time he sees me, he will salute me.

When his shoes collide, they also generate a "KA" sound.

This ghost helps me a lot.

Every time I perform the transformation of nectar water for offering:

Garuda.
All the ghosts and spirits of the wilderness.
Raksasa and Hariti.
All filled up with nectar.
Om, mu-di-yu, so ha. Om, mu-di-yu, so ha. Om, mu-di-yu, so-ha.

This American soldier ghost helps to maintain order for those coming to receive my nectar offering.

There was once a wandering mangy ghost who wanted to stay in "New South Mountain Retreat." But, as he had a bad temperament, he was considered unqualified by the American soldier ghost who pulled him out and made him leave.

In fact, there are also ghosts at "True Buddha Quarter," but these ghosts are my disciples who took refuge in me. They are very good; they know how to cultivate Vajrayana Dharma and help me a lot. All the ghosts in "True Buddha Quarter" can fly and make supernatural transformation. They are already getting close to being "gods."

I asked them, "Is it good being a ghost?"

They answered, "Good!"

"How is it good?" I asked.

The group of ghosts said, "A ghost has neither form nor body, just spirit. No form or body results in less sickness and affliction. We all have a little bit of supernatural power, are able to transform and fly, and can go anywhere we please. There is so much freedom and we do not want to be bounded by the physical form, which would be very troublesome."

I said, "Ghosts may reincarnate again to become human beings."

The group of ghosts answered, "Only a few reincarnate to become human beings due to affinity and karma. In fact, human beings are ghosts and ghosts are human beings; the only difference between them is that one has a physical body and the other does not have. We are happier without the physical body."

Once, I was going out.

A ghost said, "Remember to bring an umbrella!"

"It is really sunny, why bring umbrella?" I was puzzled.

"It will rain at three o'clock in the afternoon!" the ghost said.

Sure enough, in the afternoon, the sky turned dark.

Three o'clock in the afternoon, the rain started pouring.

The ghost had predicted accurately.

I asked, "How did you know?"

The ghost answered, "Did you not say that ghosts have five supernatural powers?"

Let me tell you: we should all believe that ghosts, gods, bodhisattvas, and buddhas exist.

Sheng-yen Lu

3. The Ghost Who Hid Jewelry

It is well known that Grand Master Lu makes friends with, corresponds with, communicates with, and interacts cordially with ghosts.

One day, an old female ghost leisurely arrived.

This ghost wore a stiff and blank facial expression, looked extremely lonely, and did not speak. She just pointed to her heart.

I asked, "Is something on your mind?"

She nodded.

She wanted me to go with her and also to take me with her. Actually, I was quite unwilling, but, since a skillful man is a bold man, I went ahead without much hesitation. Perhaps, her daughter is a beautiful female ghost!

We walked into a house.

She pointed at a wooden pillar underneath a round table.

She said, "Open."

The wooden pillar separated, and in the hollow space within, there was a large stash of jewelry. My eyes lit up at the sight:

Diamond rings and diamonds.

Gold.
Pearl necklaces.
Other jewelry.
Jade bracelets.

The jewelry was in a big bag hidden in the hollow part of the table pillar, which was a perfect place for hiding the jewelry.

I asked, "Are they for me?" I was so elated.

She answered, "No! They are for my descendants!"

This time, it was my turn to wear a stiff facial expression.

After a few days, the Zhuang family came to my place and indicated their request for help:

When the old grandmother was alive, she had a large quantity of jewelry, which included gold, silver, diamonds, and pearls. After she passed away, the jewelry disappeared. When she was alive, the old grandmother had a habit of hiding things because she was afraid of being robbed or stolen from by thieves.

Her habit included hiding things in the:

"Ceiling."
"Basement."
"Back of the plated plaque."
"Freezer."
"Sofa."
"Toilet."
"Belly of the Maitreya Buddha Statue."
"Bottom of the bed."
"Pillow case."
Etc…

Due to her sudden death, she had no time to say or explain, and none of the descendants were aware of the whereabouts of the jewelry. Hence, we especially came to seek help from Grand Master Lu to find out the exact location of old grandmother's jewelry.

I thought to myself, "They have eventually come!"

Disciple Zhuang said, "If we are able to find the jewelry, we will donate to Sheng-Yen Lu Foundation. We will definitely do it."

I thought to myself, "That's more like it!"

I asked, "Have you searched everywhere?"

"Yes, we have searched numerous times; all the possible hiding places from the ceiling to the basement, including the belly of the Maitreya Bodhisattva statue."

I said, "Inside the hollow wooden pillar of the round table."

After they went home and searched, they really found it.

Disciple Zhuang asked me, "Grand Master Lu, how did you know?"

I said, "Your old grandmother personally came and told me."

"Wow! So accurate!"

Let me tell you: we should all believe that ghosts, gods, bodhisattvas, and buddhas exist.

Isn't it strange to find a face in the lake?

Sheng-yen Lu

4. The Water God of "Lake Sammamish"

When I was staying in "True Buddha Quarter," I frequently visited Lake Sammamish, which is the second biggest lake in Washington State.

I once wrote a book, "The Inner World of the Lake," that featured all kinds of stories about this lake.

At one time:

I went to the lake's pier at the small park. At the pier, there were wooden boards floating and extending onto the lake.

I went to the very end of the pier looking at the water plants at the bottom of the lake. Above the water plants, fish swam back and forth. I always enjoy watching the fish; they are always happy, and my mind will become happy afterwards.

Suddenly, I discerned gradual changes happening before my very eyes—two big eyes staring at me from the bottom of the lake.

There were also dense eyebrows, a nose, and very thick lips.

Beard covered the whole face.

I was astonished; the first thought that came to mind was illusion.

I took a look at the trees in the park, then at the mountains opposite me, and then I looked at the bottom of the lake again.

Oh heavens! That face was still there, and the two big eyes were still staring at me and sizing me up.

Isn't it strange to find a face in the lake?

Later, I meditated under a big tree beside the lake.

In my meditation, I saw a man walk towards me. It was the same big-bearded strange visitor from the lake. He started to ask me, "You can see me?"

I answered, "I can see you."

He said, "I can see that your eyes are different from other people's. Brilliance radiates from your eyes. Are they Yin Yang Eyes?"

I said, "No, mine are Divine Eyes."

He was obviously very glad to know someone could really see him. He was very polite and started to chat with me.

He said that during one winter, the snow was so heavy that he lost control of his car, the brakes failed, and his car skidded all the way down to the bottom of the lake.

He then became a water ghost.

He asked me, "Are you afraid of water ghosts?"

I replied, "I am not afraid since I am a cultivator."

He had a big laugh.

He told me that after he died, he realized that there were quite a lot of water ghosts in Lake Sammamish. Since he had a sturdy physique, the other water ghosts nominated him to be their ghost king. Not long after, he became the leader of all the water ghosts in Lake Sammamish.

One year, a heavy snowfall also caused another car to skid into the lake. All the ghosts were gladly awaiting for a new ghost's imminent arrival. However, the ghost king suddenly became merciful and commanded a group of ghosts to hold up the sinking car, open the car door, and let the person escape. They even helped him swim up to the shore, and that person miraculously survived.

I said, "Indeed you also have a compassionate heart!"

He said, "There are ghosts that are harmless to people." He continued saying, "I feel that doing this is great; continuously saving quite a number of people. Eventually the heavens became aware of this and promoted me from ghost king to water god."

I congratulated him.

He mentioned that he could also radiate lights and fly. Even though he was a water god, he could also travel in the human world.

I asked him, "Would you still want to be a human being?"

He answered, "Human beings! There are few who save and more who harm others. I don't want to be a human being."

After I listened to this, I could not help but feel affected.

The soul itself has no form. But, by attaching to an animal's body which has form, it is then able to come back and let people witness its return.

Sheng-yen Lu

5. Ghost on Your Shoulder

There was a lady named Luo Shanan who asked me, "My father was very fond of me when he was alive. Before he died, he whispered in my ear that he would certainly come back to see me after his death. But until now, why do I still not feel anything?"

I answered, "Your father had definitely come back to see you!"

"No?"

I said, "He was perched on your shoulder, why do you say no?"

"Oh!" Miss Luo Shanan exclaimed surprisingly.

Miss Luo said, "There was a strange thing that happened at the eulogy ceremony. Halfway through the ceremony, suddenly, for no reason, a bird flew in and kept making chirping sounds. At last, it landed on my shoulder and stayed there for a long time. It was reluctant to leave. It also used its beak to affectionately peck at my collar. Was this my father coming back to see me?"

I said, "Correct!"

I told Miss Luo, "The bird was the transformation of your father. He has already fulfilled his promise of coming back to see you!"

"How could my father become a bird?"

I told Miss Luo, "The soul itself has no form. But, by attaching to an animal's body which has form, it is then able to come back and let people witness its return."

I told Miss Luo, "Once, I conducted a bardo deliverance ceremony for my friend. I said, 'The bardo deliverance tonight will be very special because I have received a message that all the deceased relatives and friends will gather here tonight.' "

"Are there any special indications?"

"We will know when the time comes!" I said mysteriously.

In the evening, during bardo deliverance ceremony, a large group of "water ants" flew in from outside and these "water ants" could fly with a pair of large wings. It was amazing to see a flock of water ants pour in.

I said, "Do not kill the water ants!"

I said, "They are all soul-attached bodies."

One of the "water ants" flew to the top of my sutra chanting books and stayed put. It actually was my friend that passed away recently.

I said to the "water ant," "You can understand my words. If you are my friend, fly to the white candle and circle around three times."

That "water ant" was really obedient. It flew to the white candle and circled around three times above it.

Of all the participants of the bardo deliverance ceremony, there was not one that was not deeply amazed at what they saw.

I told Miss Luo, in the past, Marpa, the Vajrayana Kagyu Lineage Master, reversed the sequence of worship, and this resulted in the death of one of his sons.

When his son fell down from riding a horse and died, Marpa used the magic of "The Yoga of Forceful Projection" and attached the soul of his son to the body of a big bird which was commanded to fly to India to search for an honorable couple.

Marpa's son then reincarnated and was reborn.

(This story is widely circulated in Tibetan Vajrayana.)

I said:

People die and become ghosts.

Ghosts can return.

Return on the top of the altar.

Do not rashly kill a ghost-attached animal on the altar, because the deceased person might be attaching itself to the body of the animal.

After Miss Luo's father passed away, his soul attached to the body of a little bird which flew into the mourning hall and stood on the shoulder of Miss Luo. This is the truth about souls, believe it or not?

The defects caused by suicide, even after reincarnation, will carry forward to the next life as damage is already done.

Sheng-yen Lu

6. A Clinic for Suicide Ghosts

I am not hesitant to say that my younger brother, "Lu Zhaorong," committed suicide.

He had been coddled since he was small.

A child who is too well taken care of by the parents, would often become part of the "Strawberry Generation" when they grow up, and are very fragile physically and mentally.

In junior high school, he was lured by a younger female schoolmate to sniff "Super Glue" and lived his days in hallucination.

He did not wake up to reality even after the younger female schoolmate committed suicide.

After he graduated from vocational high school, he worked in a glass manufacturing factory, still sniffing "Super Glue." Even though his girlfriend tried to stop him, he did not listen. Eventually they broke up.

My youngest brother, who was my only brother, suffered such a big blow that he committed suicide by taking potassium cyanide.

His throat was completely burnt. In an instant, his soul departed from his body.

At that time, I was already in the United States.

My youngest brother became a suicide ghost and followed my mother to my home in the United States. He manifested three times in one night.

1. To show to my mother who was still alive at that time;
2. To show to Master Lianxiang and ask for money;
3. To show to me to treat his "throat."

I applied the secret practice of "Surupakaya Tathagata" with the aid of 'qi' to help my brother. It was really marvelous that his throat could make sound and, in spite of everything, was amazingly cured.

Once this story got out, it caused an uproar in the "ghost realm."

Many suicide ghosts came to my place one after another to seek treatment, and my home actually became a clinic for suicide ghosts.

Those who took poison sought treatment for internal organs.

Those who jumped to their deaths sought treatment for broken limbs.

Those who hung themselves sought treatment for their throats.

Those who died by carbon monoxide poisoning sought treatment for their brain.

Those who drowned sought treatment for their lungs.

Etc…

One day, a very ugly female ghost manifested to me. Her skin was completely damaged due to self-immolation.

I said to her, "You need to find a dermatologist!"

She answered, "Treatment from the dermatologist was ineffective, so I have to seek Grand Master Lu."

I asked, "Why is this so?"

She replied, "Mister has the practice of 'Surupakaya Tathagata.' Accordingly, that practice will definitely cure the burnt skin on my whole body."

So, I blew 'qi' on the body of the female ghost. Every mouthful of 'qi' expelled resulted in the appearance of a piece of "wonderful skin." Two pieces appeared when I blew twice.

When I blew 'qi' onto her nipples, her face was quite embarrassed.

When I blew 'qi' onto her secret parts, her face also showed embarrassment.

The three areas were completely blown at.

Once I finished blowing 'qi,' wow! Surprisingly, this ugly female ghost became as beautiful as a heavenly fairy.

Her beauty is sufficient to turn my life as a cultivator upside down!

That beautiful-as-a-fairy female ghost, at the end, surprisingly made a vow to become my attendant. Compared to this refined fairy-like female ghost, all the beautiful girls of the human world are nothing but coarse.

Fortunately, I have practiced "White Skeleton Visualization."

Otherwise, I might have taken the female ghost to be my wife!

Frankly speaking, I like ghosts more than people. I have many ghost disciples and they also belong to the group who "chases after the Buddha." They help me in the invisible world, and sometimes, their help is even better than the tangible world's.

I can communicate with the ghosts in the ghost realm.

The ghosts also know that there is a Grand Master Lu.

Here, I still want to remind people not to commit suicide because the karmic hindrance will be much heavier after committing suicide. The defects caused by suicide, even after reincarnation, will carry forward to the next life as damage is already done.

Therefore I say, the power of karma is inconceivable!

If you bet big time because of your mesmerization with money and gold, you may lose everything.

Sheng-yen Lu

7. Numerous Casino Ghosts

For people who play mahjong, most of them will have experienced some strange occurrences. After that, they will usually say: "Ghost in the cards!"

Actually, playing mahjong requires four people. The game will not work if one player is missing. Everyone thinks that four people are playing in a mahjong session, but from my observation, there are eight people playing and four of them are ghosts. Possibly, there are even more ghosts standing on the side watching the game.

There is also another experience that will make you never forget.

New mahjong learners obviously do not know how to play and they usually play without using tactics. But, the strange thing is that new learners always win. They usually make mahjong experts scream in exasperation.

Why do new learners win?

It is simple. With the ghosts' assistance, a newcomer is being dragged into the sea of gambling and he or she becomes addicted to gambling. Then, everybody can play together!

I can see that all worldly people have the gambling nature in them. As for ghosts, they like gambling even more.

Once, I visited a casino in Southeast Asia. When I entered the casino, a bunch of ghosts screamed, "The Ghost King is here, everyone dash away!"

The bunch of ghosts really dispersed.

I grabbed a ghost and asked, "Why do you call me the Ghost King?"

The ghost answered, "The Smiling Face Ghost King is hidden at the back of your right thumb. Once he appears, we cannot compete, and you will win!"

I said, "I did not come here to gamble."

At this time, the group of ghosts gradually returned.

I asked, "Why are you gathering in the casino?"

They answered, "We work under a Voodoo master who practices some techniques to make our casino dealer win. The majority of the casinos practice the ghost technique to make customers totally lose. We take the cards and move them around in order to make the customers lose and the dealer win."

I had a big laugh after hearing that.

There was another occasion when I was in a Las Vegas casino to watch "xiu" [shows].

Unexpectedly, the Four Aunties decided to gamble.

At the gambling table, I was standing behind them chanting a mantra:

The Vajrakilaya Mantra:

"Om, bie-zha, ji-li-ji-la-ya, sha-er-wa, bi-ga-nian, bang, hum-pei."

And also Venerable Xiongtian.

Both of them are super-powerful ghost kings.

They usually scare the gambling ghosts to the extent that they flee everywhere.

The Four Aunties: Chen Zhuanfang, Wei Siyan, Jiang Guanrong, and Sun Aizhen, won on every bet. The casino dealer had to consecutively change the card distributor four times.

The manager of the casino rushed there.

The security personnel rushed there.

Every time the cards were distributed, miracles happened one after another. In every bet, the dealer was miserably defeated.

It caused a big uproar in the casino.

The opponent was at their wit's end.

(In fact, it was not because we had our good luck in the cards. It was all due to the assistance we received from the two powerful ghost kings who were manipulating the cards. The gambling ghosts collapsed to the ground. We did not lose even on one bet. The casino dealer could only laugh sadly. Again and again, they could not do anything other than to keep changing the card distributors, but the result was always the same—loss.)

Whenever I, the ancestor of the ghost king, am present, all the small ghosts must obey.

I will win.

I said, most of the casinos in Southeast Asia hire skilled masters to rear ghosts for practicing the 'Five Ghosts Transporting Technique' to make the gamblers lose.

Even Western casinos have people rearing ghosts.

Therefore, if you are not skillful enough, never go to casinos. If you bet big time because of your mesmerization with money and gold, you may lose everything. Please be extra careful, everyone! The best thing is not to gamble at all.

I only saw the the Three Saints of the Western Paradise appear in the sky, and then delivered my relative to the Western Heaven.

Sheng-yen Lu

8. Ghost Relatives in a Large Hospital

Every time I go to a large hospital, the ghosts I see are really like those in the farmers' market; they are continuously walking to and fro.

There are all kinds of ghosts in the hospital. There are children, as well as old, strong, young, male, and female ghosts. There are also ghosts in "irregular forms."

Each time I see numerous ghosts standing by a patient's bedside or outside a patient's room, I know that the patient's time is up!

Once, I pointed at the patient's room or bed and said, "Amitabha Buddha! The patient is dying very soon!"

The patient whom I was pointing at really passed away within "two hours."

People asked, "Why is that?"

I answered, "All the ghost relatives of the dying patient arrive after hearing the news. Ghosts know when to come to pick up their relative." (It is indeed really accurate!)

People asked, "Are they not being picked up by the netherworld guards?"

I answered, "Ordinary people are usually picked up by their ghost relatives. As for those picked up by netherworld guards, they have heavier karma, and are sent to hell."

At one time, while my relative was dying, she saw her deceased husband coming to pick her up. She also saw her deceased son and a group of her deceased relatives and friends.

I said, "Not good! She will become a ghost!"

I took out my mala and hung it on my relative.

As soon as it was hung on her, all the ghosts disappeared.

I only saw the the Three Saints of the Western Paradise appear in the sky, and then delivered my relative to the Western Heaven.

At the point of her death, my relative said that she could initially see the arrival of all her ghost relatives, but once my mala was hung upon her, all the ghosts disappeared and she was taken and delivered to the Western Heaven.

There was another time I saw a netherworld guard holding a hand pillory, which is used for locking up people. That netherworld guard was walking around, eventually entering an operating room. I thought the patient must be dead, and would be locked away in the middle of the operation.

Surprisingly, the one being locked up was not the patient.

It was the operation surgeon.

I could only hear a period of big confusion in the operating room.

The one who was carried out was not the patient; it was the surgeon who wore a white robe. According to what I heard, halfway through the operation, the surgeon collapsed and fainted on the ground, and unexpectedly died. They also said overwork was the cause of the surgeon's death.

I saw very clearly that the netherworld guard went in and out of the operating room.

I also saw a nurse ghost who wore a white nurse cap and a white nurse uniform.

The strange thing was, this nurse ghost walked around in the hospital, went in and out of all the patients' rooms, examined every patient, measured blood pressure, took their temperature, and kept patients warm with blankets, among many acts.

I noticed that the name tag of the nurse ghost was, "Wen Cuihua."

I asked, "Is there a nurse called Wen Cuihua in the hospital?"

The medical staff answered, "Yes, she passed away a week ago because of pancreatic cancer. Although she found out she had cancer, she had never stopped working until she died. Her spirit was very admirable."

The medical staff continued, "Every one of us in the hospital admires this nurse. She was highly responsible and often worked very hard without complaining."

I said, "I see her still working in the hospital!"

The medical staff said, "Who (what ghost) do you think you're kidding?"

I was speechless because the nurse ghost Wen Cuihua was directly facing me and laughing!

Ghosts are manipulating the world's progress in civilization, science and medicine, creative works of art, and the inventions of inventors.

Sheng-yen Lu

9. The Ghost Behind "Brother Octopus"

Remember the television announcement?

In one year, during a world soccer match, there was a "Big Octopus" of an aquarium that could predict which country's soccer team would win.

When there was a match between two countries, two square boxes were set up inside the water with the names of the two competing countries labelled on them.

When the big octopus sat on top of a particular box, that country would win.

For the first win, it was probably coincidence.

For the second win, it was maybe due to probability.

For the third win, it was probably good luck.

For the fourth win, it really surprised people.

For the fifth win, it made people feel that this was inconceivable.

...

Brother Octopus was quite "accurate" in his magical predictions.

Those losing countries really hated Brother Octopus.

They really wanted to:

"Eat octopus sashimi!"

"Stir-fry the octopus!"

"Boil the octopus for soup!"

"Slice the octopus and eat with dipping sauce!"

The losing countries wanted to eat up Brother Octopus. I had a big laugh after watching [on TV]. It was because when I was watching the television news report, I had already discovered with my Divine Eyes that there was a big ghost behind Brother Octopus.

That ghost had green eyes.

His eyeballs were continuously rolling.

His brain was quite developed with a great ability of predicting.

The prediction was so accurate because it was the ghost behind Brother Octopus manipulating him, and it had nothing to do with Brother Octopus himself!

I, Grand Master Lu, already knew and saw it. Ghosts are manipulating the world's progress in civilization, science and medicine, creative works of art, and the inventions of inventors.

You should believe:

Ghosts exist.

Gods exist.

There was a man who bought a new car.

When he drove the car, the steering wheel would tremble vigorously by itself. He went to discuss this with the car dealer company.

The car dealer agent said, "None of the cars of the same brand and same model have this kind of problem occurring. It only happens to your car."

The car dealer agent test-drove the car.

No trembling.

The owner drove.

It trembled again.

It was really strange!

The car dealer agent said, "It is our responsibility to fix your car until the steering wheel is completely not shaking."

In order to fix the car, they had to find out the cause of the problem. They did not know what to do because they could not find out any reason. When the mechanic drove the car, the steering wheel did not shake.

The car was returned to the owner.

When the car owner started the car, the steering wheel trembled again!

The car dealer agent and the mechanic were dumbfounded.

Eventually, they invited me there and I chanted, "*Om, bie-zha, ji-li-ji-la-ya, sha-er-wa, bi-ga-nian, bang, hum-pei.*"

I sprinkled water to purify the car.

I saw a ghost flee away from the steering wheel. It flew and disappeared to the south-east direction!

I said, "The steering wheel should stop shaking now!"

The car owner said, "Is that true?"

I said, "It is true."

The car owner drove the car again. He was very happy because the car was really working fine!

One needs to believe that ghosts really do exist. This is true.

With so many ghosts all appearing, it meant something big was going to happen.

Sheng-yen Lu

10. Ghost Shadows That Appeared at a Baseball Field

I was delighted to go and watch a baseball game. When I arrived at the baseball field, it was fully packed with people. This ball game really attracted thousands of people, as all the seats were filled up. Many were left standing.

Each of the two teams had its own "fensi" [fans]. The cheerleaders demonstrated all kinds of skillful techniques, and the atmosphere was extremely lively.

Flag banners, hats, and whistles appeared one after another.

I observed for a short while, then quietly departed from the field, and dared not stay long.

Why?

It was because I saw many many "ghosts" there also watching the game. I certainly realized that with these many ghosts around, there was going to be a problem. Just like the saying: "One does not visit a temple without a cause." With so many ghosts all appearing, it meant something big was going to happen.

I left!

I did not continue watching the ball game.

This is because I am a person who never stays long in "a place of trouble" and never goes to "a place of trouble."

Later!

When watched from the television, I saw that when the ball game was half way through, the players started to argue with one another due to the problem of the unfair referee. Both teams ended up fighting. The "fans" who were supporting their own teams went down to the field to join the fighting, creating a situation of two armies with clubs flailing. The situation got out of control, with many wounded in action. Some of them had fractured bones, and some were even trampled to death. It was chaotic.

People can, in an instant, lose all rationality.

Emotions boil over.

How could they be so impulsive?

My answer to this is, "When there are too many ghosts around, people will naturally lose control."

There was another occasion:

Again, it was a ball game played by celebrities. There was also a multitude of people who arrived and filled up the entire observation platform.

This time, it should be a peaceful match because not too many "ghosts" were attending.

I felt so much relieved.

I only saw one "obstacle ghost" arrive.

This "obstacle ghost" seemed to know me.

He asked, "Grand Master Lu watches the ball game?"

I answered, "I am a baseball fan."

He asked, "You don't have another purpose for coming to watch the ball game, do you?"

I answered, "What other purpose? I simply came to watch the game."

He questioned, "You will not use your power to interfere with me?"

I replied, "We do not owe each other anything, why should I interfere with you?"

The obstacle ghost said, "I feel relieved then!"

In the field, I saw the "obstacle ghost" suddenly emerge from the east, from the west, from the south, and from the north. The "obstacle ghost" was running here and there; who knows what he was doing?

At this time, as a national champion was running between bases, I saw the obstacle ghost use his body to block him. No sooner said than done, this national champion leaned forward and crushed the leg that was sliding towards the base. With a cracking sound, his leg bone broke and the tendon got twisted. He fell to the ground and was unable to get up. Eventually he was carried out of the field. It is said he could not participate in any match for a year.

The obstacle ghost was very happy.

I asked, "Why did you do that?"

The obstacle ghost replied, "That is what he (the national champion) owes me."

Even doctors and scientists were completely baffled and did not know why a healthy person would just suddenly die.

Sheng-yen Lu

11. Vampire Ghosts Spoken by Master Lianzhi

There was once a dinner gathering.

Master Lianzhi mentioned a true story about "Vampire Ghosts":

There was a fellow disciple, who had a big family.

A family member passed away, but one month after the completion of all the funeral services, another person passed away.

They thought that it was just coincidence and once again finished all the funeral services. But after twenty days later, a third person passed away.

The strange thing was, this third family member was a young person who should not have died. A sense of foreboding permeated in the family.

They hired a reverend to conduct purification and blessing ceremonies, and thought that everything should be fine. Unexpectedly, a fourth person died thereafter.

Everyone in the family was panicking. Four family members had consecutively died in less than half a year.

It was even more peculiar that a fifth person soon died!

They hired another well-experienced Voodoo master to perform the "Body Substitution Practice," and thought that with the help of a "substitute body" they could have peace in their mind.

A sixth person died yet again!

Oh my heavens! In less than a year, six family members died. Feng shui masters were hired to examine the "residence of the living" and the "burial grounds of the deceased." The feng shui masters took a brief look and made some feng shui alterations.

Once again, a seventh person died!

The family was about to go insane and crazy. Everyone was so worried that he or she will be the next in line.

Again, they hired eminent monks to conduct the "Emperor Liang Repentance," the "Great Compassion Repentance," the "Water Repentance," the "Lotus Sutra Repentance," the "Yogacara Ulka-mukha (The Ritual for Feeding of Hungry Ghosts)" the "Offering of Food to the Spirits," etc...

An eighth person died yet again!

Help! Help! [They would hire] any popular reverend, Voodoo master, feng shui master, naturalist, taoist, astrologer, supreme master, master, living buddha, exorcist, etc .....

Even doctors and scientists were completely baffled and did not know why a healthy person would just suddenly die.

A ninth person died yet again!

Oh Heavens! Oh Heavens! What else could be done?

At this time, that fellow disciple who had taken refuge in Grand Master Lu happened to remember Grand Master Lu who was living far away in Seattle, United States.

Nine family members died in a year.

Is it not scary? They were making funeral arrangements almost daily.

Once I did the divination.

The "Heavenly Official" and "Earth Killing" (Zi Wei Dou Shu) stars firmly stated that: "The paternal great-grandfather and great-grandmother were buried in a vampire land and have been transformed into vampire ghosts. Every night they fly out and absorb energy from living people, who in turn die when their energy is completely exhausted. If this continues on, more people will die."

I told Master Lianzhi to go quickly and help.

Choose a "Remove Day" afternoon to open the coffin.

Grab a handful of muddy soil and throw onto the bodies of the vampire ghosts.

This was the method to save [the living].

Master Lianzhi followed my instructions and together with a group of brave family members, went up to the grave site. When the coffin was opened, everyone was almost scared to death at the first glance!

Both great-grandfather and great-grandmother were wearing burial clothes, hats, and shoes, and they were lying there as if alive.

Hairs had grown longer. (horrible)

Finger nails had grown longer. (horrible)

Their faces looked alive with two fangs exposed. Exactly "vampire ghosts."

When everyone saw the bodies, several of them stumbled off and ran away. The remaining people followed my edict to throw the muddy soil into the coffin and closed it.

After one week, the coffin was re-opened by everyone. Amazing! Amazing! The dead bodies had already started to decompose. The clothes that were originally new and bright, were now already bitten and damaged by the insects. They really became dead bodies.

From that day onward ---

The big family was back to normal; the continuous dying events stopped happening.

I asked, "Why did you not consult me at the beginning?"

He answered, "Grand Master Lu lives so far away in Seattle, United States, and is very busy. It was when there was really no one else to consult, that I then started to remember."

12. What was Being Carried in the Motorcycle's Backseat?

One year, I returned to Taichung, Taiwan.

On a street of Taichung, I saw a True Buddha School disciple riding a motorcycle and quickly passing by in front of me.

I saw him, but he did not notice me. I saw on his back seat, a sexy girl with long hair. Dressed in a tiny outfit with legs exposed, the girl had both arms around the disciple.

I was thinking in my mind:

"Great! I could tease him tomorrow."

(He was married, had a wife, and still carried a sexy girl everywhere.)

The next day.

I asked, "Yesterday, around two o'clock in the afternoon, did you ride a motorcycle and pass by Wuquan Road?"

He answered frankly, "Grand Master, you saw me?"

I said, "Yes, who was riding in the backseat? What is your relationship with her?"

He was horrified.

I thought I had caught a "criminal."

He said, "I carried no one in the backseat!"

I questioned, "She has long hair, wears a tight mini-skirt with exposed fair legs. I saw very clearly. Her two arms were tightly entwining your waist, and you deliberately pretended not to see me."

He was greatly startled, "Grand Master, I really did not carry anyone. Could Grand Master be mistaken? Please do not falsely accuse your disciple!"

"You do not lie to Grand Master," I said.

"I dare not," he said.

At this time, I felt rather tense. This disciple never lies to people. If he said he did not carry anyone, he really meant it. But, what did I see? Could it be the "life-claiming ghost?"

I used "Divination through the Fingers." It was really a "life-claiming ghost" sitting in the backseat, I saw it using my Divine Eyes.

I had to help my disciple, I said:

Use a piece of red cloth and write down your personal eight characters of birth time, name, and address; then cut nails and hairs, wrap them all together and tie with red string.

Pick an afternoon of a "Remove Day."

Hang the pouch in front of Avalokitesvara Bodhisattva's chest.

Pray for blessing and protection.

(Then, nothing bad would happen.)

A year passed by as usual and everything was fine.

Later: On the twenty-fourth day of the first month of the new lunar year, while he was riding the motorcycle, he fell off from the motorcycle without reason. There was no accident too. He was quickly delivered to the hospital, but he died.

The doctor diagnosed that he died suddenly due to a cerebral hemorrhage (stroke).

When I heard that he had passed away, I could not believe it since he was still young.

Even though there was a "life-claiming ghost," but I had already performed a special technique and he had the protection from Avalokitesvara Bodhisattva. How could he die?

I went to his house.

I found that the shrine in his house had no red cloth pouch hanging on the chest of the principal deity, Avalokitesvara Bodhisattva.

I asked his wife, "Where is the red cloth pouch?"

His wife answered, "There was a red cloth pouch, but during the year-end cleanup, I saw the red cloth pouch was covered with dust. I took it out and threw it away!"

"Oh Heavens!" I cried.

His wife questioned, "Is his death related to the red cloth pouch?"

I answered, "That's correct!"

I explained to his wife the entire matter in detail. Now that he was taken away by the "life-claiming ghost," I must use my power to get him back and deliver him to the pure land of Maha Twin Lotus Ponds!

Yin and Yang are different, human and ghosts are unlike. You consume energy, but humans consume tangible food.

Sheng-yen Lu

13. What Foqi Lu Saw?

The father of my daughter-in-law Shanshan Lu had passed away. My son, Foqi Lu, and Shanshan Lu brought back from Indonesia some of his ashes, which were placed in the lower level of the shrine, for memorial purpose.

Unexpectedly, the soul of the father-in-law returned with them and stayed in Foqi Lu's home in Seattle.

Shanshan Lu could sense it.

Foqi Lu could sense it.

For example:

Shanshan Lu could sense that her father was sleeping in the middle of two people, between Foqi and herself.

Both of them would frequently and suddenly wake up in the middle of the night and sense that a third party existed in the bedroom.

There was one time in the middle of the night.

Foqi Lu suddenly woke up and took a look at Shanshan Lu who was sleeping beside him. He was so shocked by this glance.

It was because the face of Shanshan Lu had turned into the face of his father-in-law.

He let out a startled cry!

There was another time.

Foqi Lu awoke in the middle of the night and saw his father-in-law floating in the space above and gradually moving closer towards him. Foqi Lu was greatly alarmed and involuntarily chanted from his mouth, "*Om, gu-ru, lian-sheng, sid-dhi, hum.*"

At the same time, he pushed both hands out.

Both hands manifested a ray of white light that radiated out and forced his father-in-law to retreat. Instantly, he disappeared.

And more:

...

The occurrences of this kind of "supernatural phenomenon" were quite frequent. He was Shanshan Lu's father, Foqi Lu's father-in-law, and our relative. But, the frequency of these occurrences was too high and was affecting their normal life.

The young couple told me about it.

I went to their home and performed water purification. Wherever I sprinkled the purified water, he quickly shunned away. I completely purified the whole house.

He was forced to move outside the house.

He said, "Master Lu (in-law), I cannot live outside. If I ever get seen by the Day Patrol God and the Night Patrol God, I will be taken away."

I said, "Souls return to souls, dust returns to dust. You go to find your own destiny!"

He said, "I wish to look after my daughter Shanshan Lu."

I said, "I understand that you want to protect your daughter, but their ordinary daily life will be affected if it is too obvious. It would be better if I deliver you to the Buddha pure land!"

He said, "I am not familiar and I am afraid. I do not want to go."

(He was a Catholic when he was alive, but he was not a staunch practitioner. He could neither go to heaven nor hell.)

I asked, "Where do you want to go?"

He replied, “Stay beside Shanshan!”

I said, “I will transform the exquisite seven-layer pagoda into a house for you, and you can live in there! Remember, remain invisible as you are invisible. You cannot manifest to anyone anymore. Yin and Yang are different, human and ghosts are unlike. You consume energy, but humans consume tangible food. They provide offerings to you and you bless them. You also cannot affect my grandson Luhong and granddaughter Lujun. Would that be fine?”

He answered, “Fine!”

From then on, the soul of the father-in-law never appeared again!

The god of rain and god of wind all listened to my commands.

Sheng-yen Lu

14. The Great Ceremony Held on the Beach

I conducted the "Animal Release Ritual" on November 13, 2011 at half past one in the afternoon on the beach of Wushi Harbor of Toucheng Township, Yilan County.

This extra large outdoor "beach" ceremony was organized by:

Master Lianyue.

Master Lianmiao.

Master Liandeng.

Dharma sister Zou Yilan.

Toucheng Township Mayor. (Chen Xiuyuan).

This was also the first time in my life conducting a large ceremony on a beach facing the sea and "Turtle Hill Island"; it was really unprecedented.

Its characteristics were:

An extra high "dharma platform" was built on the beach, with its first-class sound and lighting features. (Also included were the Taiko Divine Drum and Nine Heavens Divine Drum.)

On the dragon side of the beach, a "Kalachakra" sand mandala was set up with extraordinary grandeur.

In front of Kalachakra, a statue of "Golden Mother of the Jade

Pond" was vividly crafted using sand mandala.

There were altogether thirty-three stacks of little sand mandalas in the surrounding symbolizing Indra's Heaven, with thirty-three gods.

Fish fry were directly released into the sea in relay style. These kinds of fish fry belong to the same kind of fish which are richly produced in Wushi Harbor. Thus, the "same kind" entered into the "same kind."

The miracle was:

Wushi Harbor had heavy rainfall continuously for over half a month, there was not one day without heavy rainfall, the rain stopped only on the day of the ceremony. After the ceremony finished, the rain continued once again non-stop.

Wushi Harbor had very strong gusts of wind everyday with wind speeds of around level eight to ten. When I was seated at my dharma throne, I called, "Wind stop."

The gusty wind stopped at once.

I (Living Buddha Lian-sheng), really can call upon the wind and rain.

I called the rain to stop, the rain really stopped.

I called the wind to stop, the wind really ceased.

This was another big miracle. The god of rain and god of wind all listened to my commands.

Does everyone still remember the "Mahamayuri" ceremony held at Taiwan Lei Zang Temple?

"The Great Sun! Are you going to shine on my disciples until their skin peels off? Mahamayuri, please extend your two wings to cover the sun a bit!"

It was only a short while, two pieces of huge black clouds, like birds' wings, covered the sky above the ceremony site, and bursts of cool wind blew in, helping the attendees to feel relaxed and refreshed. (The clouds only appeared at the sky above the Lei Zang Temple.)

I said, "Clouds come."

Clouds came!

And during the big drought in Indonesia, there were five months without rain.

I was at the site of the "Senayan" great ceremony.

I exclaimed, "Rain come!"

Fifteen minutes after the ceremony completed, pouring rain arrived all over Indonesia. Indonesia includes the Thousand Islands. The Thousand Islands were all covered with rainfalls and the drought was resolved.

(This scenario was reported by "Dongxie Magazine.")

I truly tell everyone:

My ancestor Jiang Ziya was gifted with the "Almond Yellow Flag" by Yuanshi Tianzun, the Celestial Venerable of the Primordial Beginning, for calling support from all gods.

Once the "Almond Yellow Flag" is waved, all the gods from heaven and earth will follow the commands.

I did not have the "Almond Yellow Flag."

But I have:

"Shakyamuni Buddha's Edict." (King of Buddhas)

"Ksitigarbha's Edict." (King of the Earth)

"Golden Mother of the Jade Pond's Edict." (King of Immortals)

These three Great Edicts could command all gods and ghosts.

In front of his bed, I opened my father's heavenly gate which was directly connected to the Buddha pure land.

Sheng-yen Lu

15. The Rebirth of My Father

My father Lu Ershun was critically ill while I was still in Seattle of the United States around October to the beginning of November of 2011.

Originally, I was scheduled to rush back to Taiwan to see him.

Golden Mother of the Jade Pond said, "You can continue with your preaching schedule. We will be guarding your father and waiting for your return to Taiwan to see him one last time, and then your father will be delivered."

After I paid homage to "Golden Mother of the Jade Pond," I went out of the main hall and prayed in front of the heavenly incense burner.

This time, Avalokitesvara Bodhisattva manifested and told me, "Do not worry, Golden Mother and I will personally return to Taiwan and deliver your father to the Buddha pure land."

I felt greatly relieved once I heard that.

I returned to Taiwan on the 3rd of November at seven o'clock in the morning and on the same day, I immediately rushed to the hospital to visit.

I used my Vajrayana method of "Consciousness Transference Yoga."

Open the gate to heaven.
Close the door to earth.
Block the path to human rebirth.
Obstruct the ghost road.

In front of his bed, I opened my father's heavenly gate which was directly connected to the Buddha pure land.

Not to be reborn in the realm of hell, hungry ghost, or animal.

Not to be reborn in the realm of human.

Not to be reborn in the realm of ghost.

(In this way, I then felt that everything was assured.)

I returned to Taiwan on the 3rd of November. Only three days after, on the 6th of November, my father was reborn to the Buddha land.

During cremation:

The cremation produced one piece of Vajra sarira, four pieces of medium-sized sariras, and numerous small sariras.

There were innumerable sarira flowers.

(Note: It was my mother, Lu Yunu, who delivered my father to the Buddha land. Through cultivation, she had already become Avalokitesvara Bodhisattva.)

When my father Lu Ershun was still alive, he had a strong character and did not believe in anything. I had considerable difficulties converting him.

Until he was old and weak, did he gradually initiate the mind of learning Buddhism.

Every time I returned to Taiwan or in the year 2010 when I stayed in Taiwan for a year, my father would always attend every one of my ceremonies.

He became part of the "Chasing After the Buddha" Group.

He received empowerment from every deity.

He always chanted the the holy epithet of "*Namo Guan Shi Yin Pu Sa.*"

The Buddha seed was already planted.

Now, it is just waiting to grow big and strong.

Reverend Liandeng interviewed him and asked, "You are the father of Living Buddha Lian-sheng Sheng-yen Lu, why do you pay homage to your son?"

My father replied, "I am not paying homage to my son. Rather, I am paying homage to the Tathagata's Wisdom of my son, which represents paying homage to Tathagata's Thusness. In this way, can you understand?"

After my father was reborn, he returned to see me once. He woke me up by touching my feet.

My father appeared in the space, carried a smile on his face and was coruscated with holy lights.

I am very thankful to everyone who had looked after him:

Xiao Zhang.

Wang Zizhu.

Xu Hongchun couple.

Doctor Li Jialin.

Doctor Xie.

Reverend Lianxing.

Master Lezhi.

My four younger sisters and their husbands.

The immediate relatives of Shimu.

Vice President Shi of China Medical University Hospital.

...

If there was a difficult problem, I would then write a note petitioning, "City God, please help!"

Sheng-yen Lu

16. The City God and I are Good Friends

I was born at the Niuchou riverbank of "Back Lake" of Chiayi. In the year of 1945, the American army aircrafts bombed Chiayi. My parents fled and stayed at the chicken farm at Niuchou River and I was born at the chicken house.

Coincidentally:

"Jesus" was born in the stable.

"Sheng-yen Lu" was born in the chicken house.

I was a premature baby and therefore difficult to raise. I was adopted by the "City God" of Chiayi as his godson.

That means when I was born, the "City God" deities and I had formed a virtuous affinity.

Excellent!

Excellent!

Later on, I understood that "City God" was differentiated by numerous rankings:

Capital City God.

Prefectural City God.

County City God.

Village City God.
(There is even a small City God in Tainan.)
After my Divine Eyes were initiated, the "City God" of Zhongxiao Road in Taichung and I became close friends.
I remembered when I was at Buddhist Lotus Society of Minsheng Road in Taichung, there were several Buddhist friends such as "Lay Practitioner Yuan," "Lay Practitioner Jiang," and "Lay Practitioner Wen," and so on, who knew I had psychic power and consulted me on certain matters.
I calmed my mind.
I could see a person descending from the space, wearing a red robe, crowned with a black hat [worn by feudal officials], his appearance upright and dignified. He was, without a doubt, the City God of Taichung.
One by one, the lay practitioners asked their questions.
I asked the City God.
The City God replied one after another.
The lay practitioners gave the thumbs-up. They shouted, "The divination is so accurate!"
At that time, I was in Taichung helping people out with their questions by providing consultations. If there was a difficult problem, I would then write a note petitioning, "City God, please help!"
The person who came for consultation would then take the note to the City God temple and burn it together with joss paper.
Matters would then be resolved.
Do you find it strange or not.
When I taught the "Practice of Praying for a Son," it was also done by praying to the City God in Taichung. In that year, who knows how many were successful in obtaining a son by this Practice of Praying for a Son from the Taichung City God?
In that year, the "Hat of City God" could cure lots of hard-to-treat illnesses. Take the Hat of City God, put it on the head of the patient

three times, and surprisingly the sicknesses would bizarrely be cured.

Isn't it strange?

At that time, I was still in the army.

Everyone is very familiar with the incident of Deputy Commander Wei Qingping. Let me repeat one more time here:

Wei Qingping and I went to "Gongbei Mountain" of Penghu County to do land surveying.

Wei was holding some copper coins and said to me, "Survey Officer Lu, I have some copper coins clenched in my fist. You say you can perform divination. I will believe you if you can guess right. Otherwise, from now on, please do not talk about Buddhist dharma in the army!"

I was provoked.

I could only calm my mind.

At this time, the City God of Penghu came and told me, "Fourteen pieces."

I answered, "Fourteen pieces."

Deputy Commander Wei Qingping opened his palm and counted the copper coins. When he counted to thirteen pieces, only one piece was left on his hand. The final count was precisely fourteen pieces.

Wei Qingping said, "I believe you now!"

From then on, Wei Qingping chanted the Buddha's name continuously until today. He has been my witness twice; once at Taoyuan Stadium, the other at Taiwan Lei Zang Temple.

I truly tell everyone, the fact that I am friends with gods is real.

The size of the Bodhisattvas does not correlate to the strength of divine efficacy.

Ksitigarbha Bodhisattva

17. Thirty-six Small Statues of Ksitigarbha Bodhisattva

Ksitigarbha Bodhisattva and I have a profound affinity. He frequently appears in my writings. He is my big brother and I address him as "Big Brother Ksitigarbha."

Sometimes we are like close friends and can talk about anything. We are like glue and paint, there is no distinction between the two of us.

Sometimes we are like father and son.

He is one of my three principal deities, "The Great Vow Ksitigarbha Bodhisattva."

Ksitigarbha Bodhisattva is very good to me. Good to an extreme degree. Moreover, I can go to Ksitigarbha Bodhisattva's pure land "Cui Wei Pure Land." It seems like I am the only one who can go there.

Besides, Ksitigarbha Bodhisattva commanded one of his ten Great Ghost Kings, the "Smiling Face Ghost King," to accompany me and protect me while I preach in the mundane world. Some of the vicious ghosts and demons, once they see the appearance of the "Smiling Face Ghost King," will immediately escape. The "Smiling Face Ghost King" is hidden in my right thumb. My thumbprint bears the appearance of the "Smiling Face Ghost King."

There was one evening.

Thirty-six small statues of Ksitigarbha Bodhisattva suddenly appeared. These thirty-six statues wore the same facial expression and the Five Buddha Crown; each statue held a monk's staff in one hand and a precious pearl in the other hand. Each of them sat on "Diting, the Unicorn Beast."

They told me, "Master Lu, you must release us, you must, you must."

I was astonished, "What is going on?"

The thirty-six Ksitigarbha statues said together, "You will know tomorrow, be sure to release us."

The next day, I was invited by a Buddhist temple to examine the geography of the temple. The scale of this Buddhist temple was not small, and could be considered as magnificent.

The abbot said, "This temple was quite small originally. Later on, since the response to prayers was efficacious, the local people raised money to build a big temple. I then became the abbot. However, contrary to expectations, after the big temple was built, fewer people came to offer incense. With fewer pilgrims coming, the front courtyard became desolate."

I went into every hall to pay homage.

When I arrived at the Ksitigarbha hall pagoda, I saw a huge gold-plated standing Ksitigarbha Bodhisattva statue.

I asked, "The temple is well established, why is it not prosperous?"

Ksitigarbha Bodhisattva replied, "Just waiting for Master Lu to arrive, then it will be prosperous."

I asked, "Why is that?"

Ksitigarbha Bodhisattva answered, "In the past, the temple was small but very prosperous; today, the temple is big but declining. It is because people do not understand the reason behind rise and fall and do not trace back to how it originated. The original thirty-six small

Ksitigarbha Bodhisattva statues were abandoned in the storage room with nobody worshipping, and that is the reason for the decline."

I questioned, "Are the thirty-six small Ksitigarbha Bodhisattva statues that important?"

He answered, "The temple was small, but full of spiritual responses because of the spiritual response power of the small Ksitigarbhas; once the big temple was built, those thirty-six small statues of Ksitigarbha were all abandoned in the storage room, how could the temple avoid declining?"

I asked, "Are not the current Buddhas and Bodhisattvas much bigger and more stately?"

He answered, "The size of the Bodhisattvas does not correlate to the strength of divine efficacy."

I asked the abbot, "You locked up all the thirty-six small statues of Ksitigarbha Bodhisattva which hailed from the founding days of the [small] temple, is that right?"

The abbot replied, "I do not know. My predecessor relocated the small statues of the Bodhisattva since he felt we already have the big statues. I do not know where they are now located."

I said, "Storage room."

The abbot led me to the storage room. Once opened, a moldy smell struck my nose. Spider webs and dust were everywhere, and junk was all piled up. The small Ksitigarbhas were found among the junk. After counting, it was exactly thirty-six statues.

The abbot exclaimed in astonishment, "Master Lu is really amazing!"

It was because Xuan Tian Shang Di, the Devil-Sweeping Celestial Venerable of the North Pole, wanted to protect the little girl, I did not even inform her mother nor anybody else.

Sheng-yen Lu

18. Xuan Tian Shang Di, the Devil-Sweeping Celestial Venerable of the North Pole

One day at the Seattle Lei Zang Temple of the United States. A young girl from California, seemed to be "possessed," which meant being invaded by a "Strange Spirit."

If everyone had seen the movie "Exorcist," then it could be understood what this was about.

She was a fair and delicate-looking girl. Her face was suddenly changed and she looked completely like a different person.

The face had a sinister twist.

The eyes had a savage glint.

The tongue stuck out from the open mouth.

The dense white teeth wanted to bite people.

Everyone felt fear when they saw this, and dodged her.

Only Grand Master Lu leisurely formed the "Five Lightning Mudra," blew a breath, and released the "Lightning Mudra."

A "boom" sound rang and the little girl who was originally baring her teeth and brandishing her claws and running towards me, suddenly fell on the ground and vomited white foam. After a while, she woke up and was back to her usual fair and delicate-looking self.

Everyone applauded.

However, after a short while, the "Strange Spirit" once again "possessed" the girl, and her face changed to that of a flesh-biting ghost. She pounced towards me.

This time round, I was not going to be courteous, and the "Smiling Face Ghost King" appeared. Both my hands formed the "Flying Wheel Mudra" and circled it above the head of the little girl who continuously cried, "I dare not do it anymore! I dare not do it anymore!"

"Plonk." She fell on the ground again.

The "Strange Spirit" really ran away.

This time, the little girl recovered to become a normal person, and the strange spirit no longer possessed her body anymore.

The mother who brought the little girl repeatedly asked me, "What to do? What to do? When she returns to California, she will be possessed by the strange spirit again. What are we going to do?"

I contemplated seriously...

I heard a voice saying, "Grand Master Lu! I can take care of this matter, everything will naturally be resolved."

I looked up at the shrine ---

On the shrine, there was a statue who wore a general's crown and an armor; his right hand held a double-edged sword and his feet rested on a tortoise and a snake. This holy statue was radiating with fine lights. It was him who opened his mouth talking.

He was:

"Xuan Tian Shang Di, the Devil-Sweeping Celestial Venerable of the North Pole."

I took a look, and then said, "Excellent! Excellent! The little girl will be saved!"

I drew a "Shang Yan" talisman and blessed the little girl again.

It was reported that after returning to California, the little girl's "possessions" became fewer and fewer, and eventually she became completely normal.

One day, they returned to "Seattle Lei Zang Temple" again. They especially returned to thank all the Buddhas and Bodhisattvas.

The little girl pointed to Xuan Tian Shang Di, the Devil-Sweeping Celestial Venerable of the North Pole and said, "It was this Venerable who saved me."

I secretly said in my mind, "Really accurate!"

It was because Xuan Tian Shang Di, the Devil-Sweeping Celestial Venerable of the North Pole, wanted to protect the little girl, I did not even inform her mother nor anybody else.

Later on:

The little girl specifically pointed out that that the God who saved her was exactly "Xuan Tian Shang Di, the Devil Sweeping Celestial Venerable of the North Pole."

This is absolutely "Yogic Response."

(Initially, when the little girl was possessed, the family had searched through all the temples, palaces, and churches in California, and looked for all the famous doctors and psychics, but there was no hope for cure. Great reverends, living buddhas, masters, Taoist masters, spirit mediums, etc… All said, "It is incurable." Later on, when they heard that I was in Seattle and wanted to find me, the Great Reverend said, "It is also useless to find Sheng-Yen Lu, since my power is stronger than Sheng-Yen Lu's." Well, the result is for all to witness!)

I, Grand Master Lu, actually dare not boast the strength of my own powers. I only go with the natural flow of things to save sentient beings. "The decree is with me, all gods will come to help."

Buddhas do not say false words!

Sheng-yen Lu

19. Spoken Words Become Efficacious

There was a Hong Kong entrepreneur, dharma brother Zheng, who researched on his own and invented many exquisite Vajrayana dharma instruments.

There are:
Shiny beautiful malas.
Delicate body-protection amulets.
Cross vajra scepters.
Nectar treasure vases.
Smoke offering censers.
Etc…

It was needless to say that they were exquisitely made and they had an elegant quality. Every piece of work included the dignified totems such as parasols, eight auspicious symbols, and five-colored clouds. The Vajrayana dharma instruments invented by dharma brother Zheng were modular—the pieces could be disassembled and regrouped again—just like the "Transformers." We were so amazed after seeing them.

Dharma brother Zheng's dharma instruments were free gifts. He was very supportive of the "Sheng-yen Lu Foundation," so as long as you made a donation to the "Foundation" for a certain amount, you would receive dharma brother Zheng's dharma instruments as free gifts. These were very precious free gifts, as the cost of making them was not cheap. These dharma instruments had nothing to do with Brother Zheng's business. He wholeheartedly supported "True Buddha School" using his money and energy. Everything was given free, so he gave himself a monicker, "Dumb Dumb."

I laughed at him once, "At the rate you are doing this, would your company not close down eventually?"

He answered, "I am just goofing around."

Strangely enough, after I uttered my joke, "Would your company not close down," dharma brother Zheng's company, no longer received a single order. Not even one order. Without any order, what could the company's production line produce?

Dharma brother Zheng became very anxious and he found me, "After Grand Master's one phrase, 'Would your company not close down,' I do not have orders coming in. It is exactly like what you said. Grand Master, I pray to you to help and just say the golden words at your dharma throne—to let orders come to dharma brother Zheng's enterprise company!"

I asked, "Will it be like this?"

He replied ---

"Grand Master is a Buddha, Buddhas do not say false words."

That day, while I was giving a dharma talk at my dharma throne in Taiwan Lei Zang Temple, I said, "Let dharma brother Zheng's company receive orders! Let his business thrive and be prosperous!"

Strangely enough, once he returned to Hong Kong, he immediately received a big order. Currently, his business has been picking up and becoming more and more prosperous. It is really worthy of celebration. Are my words efficacious? It is really strange.

I said, "Closing down!"

The company received no order.

I said, "Thriving!"

The company's orders then arrived.

This is quite strange, does my mouth have such a strong spiritual efficacy?

And:

Three weeks before I conducted a ceremony on the beach at Wushi Harbor of Toucheng Township of Yilan County, there were heavy rainfalls every day. On the day I conducted the dharma ceremony, the rain stopped. It was the only day that the rain stopped.

I was on my dharma throne and also said, "Once the ceremony is completed, you can continue the heavy rainfall!"

I should not have said this sentence, because heavy rainfall resumed that evening.

This time, with continuous heavy rainfall in Hualian, Taitung, and Yilan counties, lots of crops were completely destroyed. There were also falling stones, mudslides, and floods. Roads were closed, streams surged, cars were covered by water to the roof, and lots of residential houses had water flooding in.

I think, I cannot arbitrarily make jokes anymore, since they become true once I open my mouth.

Buddhas do not say false words!

Water Deva, whose Sanskrit name is "Varuna," is one of the Twelve Devas in Vajrayana, one of the Guardians of the Eight Directions, protecting the Heaven in the western direction, and is the king of the dragon family.

Sheng-yen Lu

20. The Mouth of Water Deva

In November 2011, Thailand suffered from a major flood. Its loss was really immeasurable.

Three causes of the major flood were reported:

1. Abnormal weather.
2. Geographical factor.
3. Human negligence.

Abnormal weather generated the heavy rainfalls. The geographical factor was the estuary to the Pacific Ocean usually flows smoothly, but due to a period of [geographical] anomaly, the water inundated over the embankment. Human negligence was the poor water drainage facilities throughout the whole of Thailand and storm water drainage engineering to cope with flood.

Thailand was flooded, even the capital Bangkok could not avoid it. Instantly, Bangkok was thirty percent flooded, fearing that even the seventy percent would be soon flooded too.

True Buddha School has a chapter "Mi Xing Tang" in Thailand, located in Bangkok.

There was a disciple who prayed to "Padmakumara."

That night.

Grand Master Lu appeared in the dream of the disciple and said to the disciple, "You follow me!"

Grand Master brought the disciple to a place and said, "You take a look!"

That place then revealed a big crack.

All the flooding water formed into a big maelstrom and was gradually swallowed up by the big mouth of the earth crack.

On November 20, 2011, the flood in Bangkok suddenly withdrew.

The big flood had withdrawn, mysteriously withdrawn!

Originally, the city of Bangkok was supposed to be completely flooded. In the end, it was only thirty percent flooded, the rest of the seventy percent was completely normal.

The True Buddha disciples of "Mi Xing Tang" eulogized this matter of the earth cracking and swallowing the flood water.

In Thailand, I have my books published in Thai. The disciple who published my books in Thai is dharma sister Zhang Yufang. Her house was not flooded.

Excellent! Excellent!

The flood in Bangkok only covered thirty percent and then withdrew, what was going on?

Was it because the disciple prayed to "Padmakumara"?

According to my understanding:

It was "Padmakumara" who invocated "Water Deva." Water Deva, whose Sanskrit name is "Varuna," is one of the Twelve Devas in Vajrayana, one of the Guardians of the Eight Directions, protecting the Heaven in the western direction, and is the king of the dragon family.

"Water Deva" is a big God in Hinduism, is the master of all the rivers, and dominates all kinds of water for human beings.

Grand Master Lu supplicated the mouth of "Water Deva" to swallow Thailand's flood water.

I formed the "Water Deva Mudra":

I made a fist with the left hand, the thumb is not attached within the palm, index finger upright and slightly bent.

Chanted the mantra to invocate "Water Deva":

"*Namo, san-man-duo, mu-tuo-nan, ah-ban-bo-duo-ye, so-ha.*"

And:

"*Om, po-luo-na-ye, so-ha.*"

And:

"*Om, mei-tuo, shi-li, so-ha.*"

Therefore, "Water Deva" opened the big mouth and swallowed up all the big flood water.

Whoever has visited my private shrine in South Mountain Retreat, Bellevue, Seattle of the United States, already knows that I worship "Water Deva" in my private shrine.

"Water Deva" is the most beautiful deva amongst the Guardians of the Eight Directions, the Twelve Devas, and the Twenty Devas.

He lives in the middle of the ocean and stands on top of a conch.

One head, two arms.

Wearing a "hair-bundled grass crown."

The appearance is as beautiful as a fairy, with the top half of the body naked.

Fine and exquisite body curvature, half covered with heavenly cloth and layers of skirt.

All around, there are dragons, water species, and fish surrounding, with palms put together towards "Water Deva."

I, Grand Master Lu, must recite the holy name of "Water Deva" and chant the mantra of "Water Deva" in my daily cultivation.

Therefore, the mouth of "Water Deva" swallowed the flood water and saved Thailand from the disaster of flood.

The two Gods of Wealth and Merit had disappeared, and changed to a group of fierce and evil spirits.

Sheng-yen Lu

21. Two Wealth Gods Standing Guard

Once I went to a restaurant for dinner. When entering the door, I was so shocked to see that there were two Gods of Wealth and Merit (Earth Gods) standing inside the door.

I smiled and greeted the two Gods of Wealth and Merit.

"Hi! How are you?"

This time, it was the two Wealth Gods' turn to be surprised, for here was one human being who could actually see them.

The two Gods of Wealth and Merit graciously returned the greeting, "Guest, come and sit."

I heard the two Wealth Gods whispering in the restaurant,

"Who is that?"

"Master Lu, do you not know?"

"Who is this incredible being?"

"He was Padmakumara in his past life, and he delivers sentient beings this life."

"Who is Padmakumara then?"

"The transformation of Amitabha Buddha."

"Ha! His background is quite impressive, no wonder he could see us."

"He has numerous miraculous experiences."

When I listened until here, I did not want to listen anymore. I shut off my "Clairaudience."

I said to my disciple at the same table, "This restaurant will be greatly prosperous in the future!"

Later on, it really happened as I predicted, from one restaurant they expanded to two, and then three, four, and five restaurants…Business was extremely good and booming, with strong financial resources. The money was really rolling in continuously.

Why could I predict the restaurant becoming prosperous?

Because:

The restaurant had two Gods of Wealth and Merit standing guard, how could it not boom?

Many years had gone by.

I went to this restaurant again. Once I entered the door, I did not see the two Gods of Wealth and Merit; but instead, I saw several "non-human" ferocious evil ghosts running back and forth in the restaurant.

I took a deep breath.

And discovered that all were "evil energy."

Actually, I was very surprised. What was going on? The two Gods of Wealth and Merit had disappeared, and changed to a group of fierce and evil spirits.

I said to the disciple at the same table, "It is over! This restaurant is doomed to fail!"

It became true again later on!

Food in the restaurant ran into problems, hundreds of people had mass poisoning and needed to be hospitalized. The restaurant's reputation had deteriorated a great deal.

In the past, it was so busy.

Now, it is so quiet.

The big restaurant had an external renovation, the scaffolding suddenly collapsed, a number of people were killed or wounded.

Another two restaurants caught fire with no cause or reason. The fire was quite strong, people were burnt to death. The restaurants were forced to close down business.

The owner of the restaurant went to Las Vegas and lost lots of money!

The owner had misconducts. (The owner sexually assaulted somebody's wife and daughter.)

The owner of the restaurant played with stocks and got stuck in the stock market.

The shareholders became disharmonious.

Court cases one after another.

Overall, unfortunate matters happened without break. After many years' prosperity, the business was back to square one within just a few years.

One day, I met the two Gods of Wealth and Merit.

I mentioned this matter and the two gods told me what happened at the peak of the owner's business.

The company's driver was a kept man of the owner's wife. A misconduct had taken place.

The owner's misconduct was that of having three mistresses.

The restaurant's misconduct was that of knowingly serving customers expired food. They also participated in a debt collection organization, and fell into bad company.

Days and nights were spent gambling.

They robbed and seized shareholders' money.

The two Gods of Wealth and Merit could not bear to see it and then left!

Therefore, blessings were all finished!

I saw that this plot of land was actually sparkling and radiating so much brilliance that I was unable to open my eyes.

Sheng-yen Lu

22. Bought Two Small Plots of Land

When I was living in the United States of America, I bought two small plots of land. It was a sales agent who took me to see the lands and I bought them.

The first plot of land was far away from my residency. From Highway No. 5, go north, then from Exit 212, turn west and arrive at a peninsula which I called "Ke Mi Te" (Kermit). The driving time is about one and a half hours.

This land was facing the Pacific Ocean. It was where I met the "Eight Great Dragon Kings." Back then, that area was quite desolate and sparsely populated, and therefore the price was cheap. I bought it with the aim of building the "True Buddha University." (That was what I had in mind.)

The land occupied 130 acres.

I recited the Local Earth Deity mantra:

"*Namo san-man-duo, mu-tuo-nan, om, du-lu-du-lu, di-wei, suo-ha.*"

I stamped my left foot on the ground three times.

A Local Earth Deity came out.

I asked, "Can buy this land?"

He replied, "Can."

I asked, "Any profit?"

He answered, "Steady growth."

Therefore, I bought the land. It was really "steady growth," the price had gone up, but comparatively slow.

And:

Another plot of land was located at the south of my residency. From Highway 405, go south, and arrive at "Kent" district. The land occupied only thirty acres.

Back then, the surroundings of that land were equally desolate and uninhabited; it was a big piece of forest land with overgrown weeds everywhere.

There was only one supermarket in the neighbourhood, and not even one residential housing.

That plot of land was also very cheap.

I recited the Local Earth Deity mantra:

"*Namo san-man-duo, mu-tuo-nan, om, du-lu-du-lu, di-wei, suo-ha.*"

I stamped my left foot on the ground three times.

Again a Local Earth Deity came out.

I asked, "Can buy this land?"

He replied, "Can."

I asked, "Any profit?"

He did not reply, he only used his hand to draw a circle in the space, and I was very surprised once I saw it. Heavens! From the circle revealed numerous commercial avenues and shopping malls which had densely populated residential communities in the neighbourhood with busy traffic. It was a very bustling scenery.

I was shocked.

I asked, "How much will it gain?"

He answered, "Twenty times."

I bought it without a second thought.

Subsequently, it was really like that. Originally, it was a piece of desolate and uninhabited land. The government designated the land for developing a commercial district with residential communities behind it. Not even a few years, a new city had been developed. From nothing it changed to being something, and from a deserted land it changed to a prosperous place. The price of my plot of land had gone up twenty times. My God! It was really scary.

And:

One year, I passed by a plot of land.

I saw that this plot of land was actually sparkling and radiating so much brilliance that I was unable to open my eyes.

I said, "This land belongs to the world's richest man!"

(I did not have money to buy at that time.)

It became true later on. That plot of land was bought by Bill Gates for building the Microsoft company.

Bill Gates became the richest man in the world. Once again, "the divination is really accurate."

I sat in the library for a total of six hours in order to complete reciting a hundred times.

Sheng-yen Lu

23. White Lotuses Emanate from My Mouth

One day, as I passed by a large monastery, the sound of sutra recitation wafted from it, and so with curiosity, I went in.

The monastery was actually holding a ceremony. In the center, there was one person who had a shaved head and he wore a yellow cassock with a red precept robe on the outside.

Surrounding him were two rows of female lay Buddhists wearing black Haiqing robes and each of them was holding a sutra for recitation.

Behind the black Haiqing robes, there was a group of believers, not too many of them; but, they filled up the whole main hall.

I listened carefully to the scriptures of the sutra, it was the "Avalokitesvara Bodhisattva Pu Men Pin," a chapter within the *The Saddharmapundarīka Sūtra* (*The Lotus Sutra*).

The believers who were reciting and praying were very pious. Their heads were lowered; only the sound of sutra reciting was heard. There was no other sound.

There were three golden statues in the main hall and they were:

Fundamental Teacher Shakyamuni Buddha in the middle.

Medicine Vaidurya Light King Buddha on the right hand side.

Amitabha Buddha on the left hand side.

Skanda and Sangharama Dharmapalas at the left and right.

On the offering table, there was also another statue, "Avalokitesvara in Royal Ease Posture," that was made with vaidurya glass. This Avalokitesvara statue had the blue and green colors mixed together. It was very dignified and pretty. It carried the Goddess' merciful light which was [as vast as] a big ocean.

Just at that moment, I heard a sound:

"Grand Master Lu, you can recite as well."

I searched for the sound and found [the source]. Wow! The Avalokitesvara Bodhisattva on the offering table had already transformed and enlarged to fill up the whole main hall. Just like the bubbles in a bubble-blowing activity, [the scene] was transparent and colorful, both illusory and real.

I asked, "Recite which sutra?"

The Bodhisattva said, "Recite along."

I said, "Oh Bodhisattva! I have learned *Pu Men Pin* before, and I am able to sing and recite, but as I do not have the sutra text with me today, how can I recite it? I know *High King Avalokitesvara Sutra* and I know it by heart; I will just recite *High King Sutra* then!"

The Bodhisattva nodded.

I also asked, "Where do I recite the sutra?"

The Bodhisattva said, "You go to the right wing. There is a little library and nobody is in there at this moment. You can sit in the library and recite the sutra!"

I asked, "To whom shall I recite?"

The Bodhisattva answered, "You will know."

I asked, "How many times should I recite the sutra?"

The Bodhisattva replied, "A hundred times."

I said, "A hundred times? You want me to recite until my mouth is dried and lips are burnt, and I have not had lunch yet! Please forgive me! Reciting for twenty times is good enough!"

The Bodhisattva did not reply, and disappeared with a smile.

On that day, I quietened my mind and recited *High King Sutra* for a hundred times. Even though each *High King Sutra* is short, reciting a hundred times would take a rather long time. I sat in the library for a total of six hours in order to complete reciting a hundred times. (Five minutes was taken for each time; the more I recited the faster it went.)

During the time of reciting, I paid no attention to people who came in; even if people questioned me, I would not answer. I only wanted to complete this arduous task of reciting as soon as possible. I heard someone say, "This person is mumbling in his mouth, he could be insane." But, no one kicked me away. I was silently moaning about the hardship in my mind.

That night, I slept.

I saw one hundred people kneeling in front of my bed.

I asked, "What are you doing? What are you doing?"

The hundred people said, "Many thanks to Grand Master Lu for delivering the one hundred of us from the sea of bitterness of the netherworld."

"What?"

The hundred people replied, "Each time Grand Master Lu recited [the sutra], one white lotus emanated from your mouth. We rode on the lotuses and left the sea of bitterness!"

I felt deep veneration for him and immediately protected him for his trip to take up the new post.

Sheng-yen Lu

24. Forensic Doctor Yang Risong

On the evening of the 23rd of November 2011, I saw a person come to the front of my bed in my dream. This person was wearing yellow khaki pants and a white top. He had sparse salt and pepper hair. His face was quite slim and angular. As I could not recognize him, I asked him, "Who are you?"

He answered, "Yang Risong."

I said, "Yang Risong? The name sounds familiar, but I still do not know who you are."

He replied, "Forensic Doctor Yang Risong."

At this time I quickly remembered. Forensic Doctor Yang Risong, a famous autopsy expert in the Ministry of Justice, is very well-known. There were lots of rumours about him, and he had exposed the truth of many mysterious cases.

I asked, "May I know why you are looking for me?"

He replied, "I need you to accompany me on my journey!"

"What happened to you?"

"Died!"

"What was the illness?"

"Colorectal cancer."

I asked, "Why do you need me to accompany you?"

He replied, "I have to go to Japan to take up a new post, and have to pass over the ocean, but there are karmic creditors in the ocean who will hinder me. I need to rely on Grand Master Lu's Buddhadharma for protection. You know that when I saved one party, the other party would surely be offended. I was a forensic doctor, and naturally these kinds of things will happen."

"Why do you go to Japan?"

He replied, "I have affinity with Japan. I am taking the position of City God Territory Master in Japan."

I felt deep veneration for him and immediately protected him for his trip to take up the new post.

Forensic Doctor Yang Risong of Taiwan actually became the City God Territory Master of Japan.

Along the way, even though there were resentful spirits, all were just unreasonable disturbances. I protected Yang Risong using three lights, and not even one thing happened.

Yang Risong said, "Once, after examining a corpse and determining that it was suicidal; on the way home, the deceased's spirit rushed to pat my shoulder. I immediately returned to examine the corpse again, and I actually identified a suspicious point, and finally confirmed it to be homicidal. This was a tricky homicidal case, and it was purposely misrepresented as suicidal. If the corpse was not carefully inspected, one would not be able to tell otherwise."

Yang Risong said, "I was the confidential secretary of Lord Yama in my previous life, and therefore I was born in this human world as a forensic doctor. Lord Yama once even invited me for dinner!"

Yang Risong said, "There was another time when I was examining a person who committed suicide by lying across railway tracks. The initial diagnosis was suicide on the railway tracks. Later on, when it was discovered that the deceased spirit was chasing the train for taking his life, I then realized that it was another homicidal case."

I asked, "You can see as well?"

He replied, "I can see, there are gods and spirits."

I asked, "Any wrongly accused?"

He replied, "Certainly, but then, as there are gods and spirits, there will not be any mistakes. A forensic doctor's responsibility is really heavy."

I asked, "You got the disease of livor mortis [purplish red discoloration of the skin]?"

He replied, "I had too much contact with the corpses, and got infected."

When Yang Risong arrived at the Japanese territory, his whole person was completely changed—he wore a big red robe and a crown. His facial features also changed to rounded appearance and a look of righteousness permeated.

I accompanied Yang Risong on his journey, and walked for a long distance. When I woke up, I was actually still in my bed.

Garuda received Buddha's edict and became one of Buddhism's protectors.

Sheng-yen Lu

25. The God Garuda

Jia Lou Da (Garuda), is the Sanskrit name of this God and it has been translated to different Chinese names like "Jia Liu Luo," "Jia Lou Luo," "Jia Luo Luo," "Golden-Winged Bird," "Wonderful-Winged Bird," "Great Peng Golden-Winged Bird," and so on.

This God in Hinduism has limitless power; it is a very fierce big bird, and is the mount of "Lord Vishnu."

The bird form Garuda.

Angry eyes.

Sharp beak.

Both hands grasping various dragons.

The wings are made from different treasures.

Both wings could stretch to several thousand miles long.

Legend has it that:

When the wings move, it can raise a typhoon.

The thrones of various Gods vibrate.

Garudas eat dragons as their food.

The emblem of Indonesia uses "Garuda"—it is their national symbol. It originated from Hinduism's Great Roc Golden-Winged Bird.

The mantra of this God:

"*Om, jia-xi-bo, so-ha.*"

Mudra:

The thumbs of both hands are crossed, the remaining four fingers form wings facing outward and wave three times like flying.

***

When Shakyamuni Buddha was living in this world, the "Naga" dragon family begged the Buddha, "Our Dragon family is already going to be eaten up by Garuda, we pray to Buddha to save our lives!"

Therefore, Buddha summoned Garuda and the dragon family to have a reconciliatory meeting.

Garuda said, "If we do not eat dragons, what else can we eat?"

The dragons were scared to death after hearing that.

The dragon family said, "If you continue eating us, the dragon population will be exterminated, and then, what can the Garuda race eat in the future?"

Once these words came out, Garuda was stunned.

Therefore, Buddha said, "Starting from today, I will grant an edict to all Buddhist disciples. When performing the vast nectar transformation into food, Garuda will be the first one to be invoked to eat the cloud-like nectar, and this nectar is tasty, filling, and purifying. What do you think?"

Garuda was very satisfied after eating it.

Thereupon, the three parties came to an agreement. Garuda then did not eat the dragon family, and switched to eating the "cloud-like nectar."

Garuda received Buddha's edict and became one of Buddhism's protectors.

The sharp beak could expel the devils.

The claws could seize devils.

The wings could stir up the devils' throne.

The golden wings could grant fortune to sentient beings because they are made with seven precious jewels.

When Grand Master Lu performs the noon-time offering of transforming nectar into food:

The recitation is:

Garuda.
All the ghosts and spirits of the wilderness.
Raksasa and Hariti.
All filled up with nectar.
Om, mu-di-li, so-ha. Om, mu-di-li, so-ha. Om, mu-di-li, so-ha.

Sprinkle the nectar outwards.

There was one time, I saw the sun was suddenly covered up. The sky turned grey and the earth became dark, and a whirlwind ensued. I was greatly startled by the instant change.

I closed my eyes, unable to open them.

When I opened my eyes, the sun was bright in the sky, and there was no sign of strong wind. What happened to the bright sun that was covered up?

I asked the spirit officer on duty.

The spirit officer on duty replied, "It was the arrival of Garuda."

The first time my mother, Lu Yunu, made offerings to Garuda, she was given a ride by Garuda to tour the world. She was exhilarated.

Garuda has the great transcendental ability of going anywhere at will and traveling around the world at only a single thought!

Once the Earth Wealth Deity received the decree, he would not dare to disregard it because it was assigned by Grand Master Lu to take the decree to the temple of Dongyue Emperor.

Sheng-yen Lu

26. Dongyue Emperor (Dongyue Dadi)

A disciple by the surname Han came from overseas to Taiwan Lei Zang Temple to see me. He handed me a piece of paper filled up with written simplified Chinese words. Its content was as follows:

Disciple Han, divorced and was raising three children.

After the divorce, he received two million American dollars.

He had a very close friend. This friend and his wife ran a jewelry business and had several shops.

This couple were not only friends to him, but were former classmates and neighbors as well. They were very good friends who would frequently travel or have meals together and have heart-to-heart talks. Their friendship spanned more than thirty years.

The couple wanted to open another shop and invited him to join the partnership.

He joyfully agreed, and by way of "lending," gave the two million American dollars to this couple with whom he had thirty years of friendship.

In the first couple of years, interests were given to him.

Later on, interest had to be temporarily owed; as owing

accumulated, they decided to stay away. After chasing them several times for repayment, it ended with no results.

Without any clues, he resorted to hire a lawyer to serve them a legal letter to claim what they owed.

From then on, the couple broke off contact with disciple Han. Even meeting up with them was impossible. (The couple simply moved out.)

Disciple Han sorrowfully related to me that he had sunk into dire straits. He could not afford living expenses, as well as his three children's living and education expenses.

He said, "I had never doubted him as we had thirty years of friendship. He did not even write an IOU. The only evidence was the original cheque. But now, my family financial situation is getting very tight, and I do not know how to deal with it?"

I was quite deeply moved after I heard this. I said, "You have to discuss with your lawyer regarding any legal questions. The lawyer has more legal knowledge in this aspect. As for my part, I will draw a talisman and give it to you. This is a talisman for claiming debts. You take the talisman and together with joss paper, burn them at the Earth Deity temple in the afternoon of a "Success" day. It may help."

The talisman style that I drew was as follows:

According to what I understood:

Once the Earth Wealth Deity received the decree, he would not dare to disregard it because it was assigned by Grand Master Lu to take the decree to the temple of Dongyue Emperor.

Dongyue Emperor was furious, "Ox-Head and Horse-Face, quickly arrest the souls of the couple here!"

Then this couple, both simultaneously dreamed of "Ox-Head" and "Horse-Face," who in possession of arrest warrants, brought the couple to Dongyue Emperor.

Dongyue Emperor was as awe-inspiring as the mountain; he had a black face, round and wide-opened eyes. He was so powerful and stern-looking that people dared not look closely.

The couple knelt down.

In the surrounding were ghost kings, ghost soldiers, Ox-Head, Horse-Face, Qi Ye, and Ba Ye, each carrying an instrument of torture, scaring the couple to death.

Dongyue Emperor emitted a big "shout," like the thunder in the sky.

This couple immediately knocked their foreheads to the ground continuously like pounding garlic.

Instantly, they confessed the whole matter.

Dongyue Emperor said, "After returning to the living world, you have to immediately return both principal and interest. Otherwise, you will be punished to the Great Avici Hell."

The jailer took the couple to see the Great Avici Hell. They were so scared that they were trembling with fear and screamed continuously.

They kept saying, "We will not dare to do it again!"

The couple had the same dream and woke up at the same time with their whole bodies trembling in cold sweat. Thereupon, they quickly calculated the total amount of two million American dollars with interest, and delivered it to disciple Han on the same night.

The couple personally told disciple Han this matter, and disciple

Han in return recommended them to promptly take refuge from Grand Master Lu because Grand Master Lu really has immeasurable spiritual power.

Disciple Han asked, “Who is Dongyue Emperor?”

I answered, “A great ruler deity in the Netherworld. He is the same as the Emperor of Mount Tai.”

This matter happened on November 26, 2011.

27. The Answer from Heaven

I had written a book and its name was *Divination to Wow You.* This book was not meant to brag. Exactly how accurate was it? It was good enough as long as you, I, and he knew. It was actually not necessary to brag.

But worldly people are always boastful and arrogant. Nowadays it is rather difficult to find someone who is humble.

All the worldly people are:

All the articles in the world belong to Sanjiang.

Sanjiang's articles belong to my village.

My village's articles belong to my brother.

My brother learned about writing articles from me.

Anyway, all modern divinators always claim that they are number one, and other people are number two. Are they accurate? Heaven knows.

Someone asked me, "Regarding the presidential election, do you know who will be elected?" (*Dong suan* [A term frequently used in Taiwan during election. Its meaning is "Electoral Victory"])

I answered, "I know."

"Are you ironclad accurate?"

"Accurate!"

People asked, "How do you know it is accurate?"

I answered, "Mine is the answer from heaven."

(When I look up to the sky, the name of the president will appear in the sky.)

Every time I look up to the sky, it is always accurate. I only told a small number of people. When the results came out, every one of us knowingly smiled.

The recent news media fabricated a lot of stories about me, and said that I was performing divination on behalf of someone for the presidential election.

The news media denounced and laughed:

"Asking gods and ghosts rather than asking people?"

The media reporter made groundless accusations about me, and spouted nonsense.

As to whether anybody had consulted me, these were also all unrealistic talks.

The media asked me, "Did anybody consult you to perform divination for the presidential election?"

I replied, "No."

The media asked, "Who will be elected?"

I replied, "I know, but, I am not telling you."

(I secretly smiled in my mind. After all, the one who requested me to perform divination for who would be elected president was actually the media itself. I knew who would be elected, but of course I could not say who. It would create a great amount of chaos if I revealed it; moreover, if one party was identified, the other party would inevitably be offended.)

Moreover, as an "outsider" monk and cultivator like me, I do not gain any benefit should a big matter like this spread. As a true cultivator, the worldly matters would automatically require the worldly people to manage. I did not want to be well known in this world because of this.

Actually, I am already quite famous. If I announced it, it would be a big problem.

Someone asked, "Do you really know who will be elected president?"

I replied, "I know."

Someone asked, "Who is it?"

I replied, "Heaven knows! Ha ha."

The person who asked the question laughed, "Ha ha."

And I also laughed, "Ha ha."

The worldly people also laughed, "Ha ha."

This article was written on November 27, 2011. According to the presidential election poll, the difference between the two candidates was 0.4 percent, the difference was so small that it intensified the election atmosphere.

I remembered three months ago, the poll between the two presidential candidates still had a 20 percent difference! At that time, I had said "tight"!

Mr. Zeng Haitang of Zhong Tian television program division raised his big thumb and said, "Really accurate!"

This section of the road made me feel very comfortable and happy.

Sheng-yen Lu

28. The Dim Light of the Long Corridor

While I was in Taiwan, the weather in winter was cold. Around ten o'clock at night, I would usually walk on foot from the seventh phase to the fifth phase of the residential district. The walk took about forty minutes.

During the journey, I would exercise and chant.

Walking from the seventh phase to the fifth phase required passing through several high-rise buildings of the seventh phase, several sections of traffic lights, three to five small lanes, and three to four big streets. I tried to walk on the pedestrian path as much as possible.

In fact, it was impossible to walk mainly on the pedestrian path because some of the pedestrian paths were blocked by business signs.

[They were:]

Blocked by the parked scooters.

Blocked by the parked cars.

Blocked by the "voltage transformer."

Blocked by the construction work.

Blocked by the big tree.

The newly-paved pedestrian paths were fairly pleasant to walk on; while the old paths were full of pot-holes and very uneven, requiring one to walk with one foot higher than the other.

I frequently had to take a detour and walk on the asphalt road surface for scooters. All these made me cautiously walk for forty minutes.

I was used to taking "Shizheng North 2nd Road." After passing by several tall buildings, I made a turn from "Shizheng North 2nd Road," passed through a long corridor of a building, and then arrived at another big avenue.

The light of this long corridor was dimmed at ten o'clock at night. This long corridor was rather long. It was a corridor of a building. It was very quiet with no one there; I quietly walked along this long corridor. I had been walking there for quite a while and had never encountered anybody walking on this long corridor.

This long corridor belonged to one particular building. There were sculptures, high and big chandeliers, and very flat and smooth ground tiles. This section of the road made me feel very comfortable and happy.

Originally, I was walking alone.

Later on, the more I walked, the more I found something wrong.

I could feel there were two adults and three children nearby following my footsteps.

All along, I am bold and skillful. Hence, I did not bother.

I was not even afraid.

I walked mine, and they walked theirs.

While I was walking on this long corridor, I started with chanting the Buddha's epithet, or reciting *High King Sutra*, and at the end chanting "Amitabha Rebirth Mantra"...

These five spirits, initially were:

Walking behind me.

Walking around me.

Later on, they were transformed to whites stripes of light shadows dancing in front of me, just like five stripes of colored ribbons flying in the space.

I did not chant or form any mudra to get rid of them.

They also did not have any evil intentions towards me. We felt comfortable being together.

Later on they raised a question, "This cultivator, who are you? You radiate light from your body."

I replied, "I am Grand Master Lu."

They said, "Oh! It is really Grand Master Lu. We have heard a lot about you. You have a well-known reputation, no wonder your body radiates rainbow light."

I asked them back, "Who are you then?"

They replied, "In the original city planning, the seventh phase was a piece of deserted land with grass and weeds overgrown everywhere, and groups of stray dogs wandered around. In the middle, there were several ancient gravesites. We were one of the gravesites in which two adults and three children were buried; we were all grave-guarding ghosts. Later on, when the seventh phase was developed, many buildings were built, the graves and bones were completely dug up and dispersed, and we became the building-guarding ghosts. Originally, we shuttled among the empty buildings. After you came, we listened to your chanting of Buddhas' name, of mantras, and of sutras. Your light and energy rubbed off on us and we could fly freely. From then, we could accumulate energy to form a body. We have to really thank you!"

I said, "It is a casual acquaintance, and it is our affinity, so there is no need to thank me."

I also asked, "Where are you going in the future?"

They replied, "We would like to follow Grand Master Lu to cultivate."

I said, "Very good! I will accept you five ghosts to be my disciples. Follow me around, I will use my light to protect you all. Follow me on the path of cultivation!"

(I really took these five ghosts [as disciples].)

29. The Great Compassion of White Dakini

I received the empowerment of Vajrayana's "Highest Yoga Tantra" from Master Thubten Dargye. After giving me the empowerment, Master immediately explained and taught me the pith instructions of the dharma practice.

The main points of his pith instructions were:

1. Secret.
2. Offering.
3. In and out breathing.
4. Wind Practice.
5. Sensation.
6. Happiness of emptiness.
7. Realization.

Every time I visited the abode of Master Thubten Dargye, he repeatedly mentioned the importance of the pith instructions. He transmitted to me the dharma practice of Highest Yoga Tantra without holding back anything. I could see that he placed high value on it.

Every time I visited "Ching Yum Fat Kok," Master always asked me to go in first; three persons would be in the room privately:

Master, the attendant of Master, and I. At that time, I was taught the important pith instructions.

Only after dharma transmission was completed, were all my disciples then called to enter the room to pay respect to Great Grand Master Thubten Dargye.

In terms of theory and flavor of dharma, I have understood the "Highest Yoga Tantra."

But, in practical cultivation, I do not have the "Karmamudra" of the human world. I truly tell everyone:

The "Karmamudra" of Vajrayana is the supreme of the unsurpassed expedient method.

It symbolizes the secret combination of "Wisdom" and "Expedient Method."

Through the "Combination."

Our "Sensations" have the greatest benefit.

Wisdom has grown.

Brightness has grown.

Great Happiness has grown.

Our "Mind" is staying within the broad clear sky and realizing the limitless "Self Nature."

I had yogic response with "White Dakini."

I formed the mudra to invocate:

"Interlocking both hands inwardly, two index fingers extended but not touching, only forming a circle, while the two thumbs point up side by side."

(The two index fingers indicate the lotus leaves, the two thumbs are both inside the lotus flower.)

"The Mahavairocana Sutra Commentary" chapter ten states:

"White is the Bodhi Mind. Staying in this Bodhi Mind, is the dwelling place of White Dakini. This Bodhi Mind is the Buddha's Bodhi where all Buddhas are frequently born, and is also the head of the Padma Family of Buddhas."

From here, I use "Secret Words" to express as follows:

White Dakini, charming and graceful, without any false pretense, she is dignified with fragrant light as she descends.

A great white lotus flower appears in the space, its petals and pistils are soft, clean, and purified.

The body and mind of the cultivator, as if illusionary and transformed, enters into the centre of the great white lotus flower.

The body and mind of White Dakini, as if illusionary and transformed, is also in the centre of the great white lotus flower.

The bloomed great white lotus flower, gradually tightens up its lotus petals to form a lotus bud. (Unopened lotus flower.)

Both orifices merged.

Both light drops dissolved.

Both qi energies opened up.

Both channels connected.

White Dakini takes all the attainment, and empowers it into the whole body of the cultivator, from crown to feet.

From bottom to crown.

Happiness and emptiness circulate interchangeably. (Profound meditation.)

At this time, great happiness, bright light, and empty nature all appear. With complete wisdom, bright light and rainbow are intertwining, thusness and the Buddha-nature are witnessed.

This kind of state, does not exist in this "human world." That kind of great sensation experienced transcends beyond all transcendences; indeed all the Buddhas are really born from the Bodhi Mind of White Dakini.

In my Vajrayana practice, I succeeded the stages:

Action Tantra.

Conduct or Performance Tantra.

Yoga Tantra.

Highest Yoga Tantra.

Generally speaking, whenever I perform the "Offering Practice," I always truly know that masters, personal deities, and vajra protectors have descended and received my offerings.

Sheng-yen Lu

30. Did They Not Come to Receive the Offerings?

The Offering Practice of Vajrayana is an important component in Vajrayana cultivation. There are even masters saying Offering is the focal point of Vajrayana.

Lineage Master Tsongkhapa said, "The three great attainments in Vajrayana are: 1. The attainment of Mantra Chanting Accomplishment (Chi Ming). 2. The attainment of Homa (Fire Offering). 3. The attainment of Samadhi."

One of them is Homa (Fire Offering), which is the Offering Practice.

There are various types of Offering Practice in Vajrayana. I will not explain them one by one here. There are external offering, internal offering, secret offering, double secret offering (Thusness Offering), etc.

I always perform offerings when I have regular meals. That is, I offer to my:

Masters.

Personal Deities.

Vajra Protectors.

During my offerings, I certainly know whether "they" have come and accepted the offerings or not.

This "knowing" comes in different forms:

1. Seeing with one's own eyes.
2. Hearing it.
3. Telepathy.

First of all, we have to "invocate," then "blow qi," and lastly "chant" (form mudra). We visualize the transformation of all the offering items into uncountable infinite numbers—they are limitless like clouds.

Generally speaking, whenever I perform the "Offering Practice," I always truly know that masters, personal deities, and vajra protectors have descended and received my offerings. This is absolutely not a "Tiger Egg" (a Taiwanese slang for fabricated exaggeration).

One day, in October 2011, at "Rainbow Temple," I was performing offering first before I had lunch.

I invocated masters, personal deities, and vajra protectors to descend. After the first invocation, I had no response.

For the second invocation, they also did not come to receive the offerings.

For the third invocation, they did not come.

I have always invocated three times, and usually they will come.

If they come after just one invocation, it indicates joy.

If they come after two invocations, it indicates average.

If they come after three invocations, it indicates the offerings are too ordinary.

But, it is very rare to have a no-show after three invocations.

At that time, since they did not show up after three invocations, I then realized there was some problem. If the various venerables did not come to accept the offerings, then there must be something the matter with the food.

I carefully tasted the food. When I tried the plate of "or-ah!" [favorite oyster dish of the Taiwanese; the term is used to refer to a delightful local dish consisting of oysters fried in eggs served with sweet sauce], I realized that the oysters had turned rotten and stale.

No wonder the masters, personal deities, and vajra protectors did not come to receive the offerings.

I told Master Lianyin, who then instructed Reverend Lianwan, to pay special attention when opening the "or-ah."

"Or-ah" have shells.

The reverends opened the shells themselves.

There was another occasion, and everyone knows about this occasion!

A group of us went to visit Buddha's Eight Sacred Sites, located at the five-thousand-year-old city "Wa Na Na Xi" (Varanasi) on the banks of the Ganges River in India. This old city is the holy land of Hinduism. Many Hindu temples such as the temples of Brahma (God of Creation), Shiva (God of Destruction), and Vishnu (God of Protection) are all located here.

Brahma.

Shiva.

Vishnu.

In Varanasi, [the gods] carry an aura of extraordinary mysticism.

That day, we took breakfast early in the morning.

I invocated three times, and each time, the masters, personal deities, and vajra protectors did not come to receive offerings. No matter how I invocated, they did not come.

I became anxious and specially invocated again with "Heart within Heart" [mudra], but still they did not arrive.

I skipped that morning's breakfast.

There were eighteen of us who were at the breakfast table. Later on, all the seventeen fellow disciples who ate breakfast collapsed with "La Xi" [diarrhea] and the whole group rushed to the washroom. The diarrhea was very severe.

We were joking around and said, "We are finished with La Xi!" (Wa Na Na Xi) [The Chinese pronunciation of Varanasi, "Wa Na Na Xi," sounds like the phrase "finished with diarrhea!"]

Do you not say it is accurate?

31. God of Wealth and Merit Advised Me to Buy a House

Around the year of 2000, I lived in seclusion in Taichung, Taiwan. At that time, the seventh phase of the city planning district in Taichung was a desolate piece of land with overgrown weeds and wild dogs gathered together, an uninhabited countryside phenomenon.

On that piece of land, there were several erected buildings and their names were:

Lian Ju Heping.

Tian Xi.

Guoji Yinyue Ting.

Renwen Lingyu.

Xin Xue Li.

Lixing Ganxing.

Besides these six buildings, a big piece of land was still vacant. At that time, as soon as night fell, it became an unpatrolled dead-end and a heaven for wild dogs.

One time, I distributed newspapers (True Buddha News Weekly), and magazines (Enlightenment Magazine) to the Earth Deity temples in the neighborhood.

(I have a habit of collecting the already-read True Buddha News Weekly and Enlightenment Magazines. After they have accumulated for a while, I will carry and place them at the Earth Deity temples in the surrounding areas, waiting for any sentient being with the affinity to take them home to read. This is also one of the ways to save sentient beings.)

Once, as usual, I went to the Earth Deity temples again to distribute newspapers and magazines.

I arrived at the Earth Deity temple of "Taichung Seventh Phase"; this Earth Deity temple was built on a sunken land like the shape of a seashell. (I called it seashell cave.)

The God of Wealth and Merit actually manifested and said to me, "Grand Master Lu, you must buy a house! Hurry! Hurry!"

I replied, "This is a desolate piece of land not suitable for residential purpose."

The God of Wealth and Merit said again, "You must buy a house! Listen to me, you can't go wrong."

I answered, "I have no money."

The God of Wealth and Merit said, "Gather together."

In my mind, I did not plan to be a long-term resident in Taiwan; I had to return to Seattle, United States. I was only living in seclusion temporarily in Taiwan; hence, I was not persuaded.

The God of Wealth and Merit said, "You take a look! It will be like this in the future."

I took a look, "Ha"! I was so shocked.

A scenery was revealed in front of me –

Buildings mushroomed one after another (they are countless); a scenery of prosperity and brilliance was displayed.

Splendid lights.

Magnificent and spectacular architecture.

High-rise blocks.

Wonderful, artistic and beautiful style.

All buildings are luxurious homes.

The God of Wealth and Merit said, "This seventh phase area of Taichung is equivalent to the Xinyi District of Taipei."

I swallowed a mouthful of saliva and said, "Good enough! I will see."

At that time, I looked through all six buildings. "Lian Ju Heping" was comparatively expensive at one hundred ninety thousand per ping [unit of area equivalent to approximately 3.3058 square meters (used in Japan and Taiwan)]. "Lixing Ganxing" was comparatively more expensive, though the difference was not much. The price of Tian Xi, Yinyue Ting, Renwen Lingyu, and Xin Xue Li were more or less the same.

When I stood in front of one of those buildings, the salesman asked us to buy.

I took out copper coins—divination standard for accuracy; I faced towards the direction of the temple and requested help from the Earth Deity. I asked if it was good to buy or not.

Three *shengbei* [a sacred combination indicating affirmative], confirmed that I could proceed to purchase.

I showed the three *shengbei* to Shimu, Master Lianxiang, to prove to her that the God of Wealth and Merit really told me to buy the house.

We eventually bought the house!

Based on the price in year 2000, the selling price in year 2010 had risen five times. (Within ten years, the price had gone up five times.)

I am very thankful to the God of Wealth and Merit who actually told me to buy the house. Although the God of Wealth and Merit is the lowest-grade god according to the divinity ranks, yet, small gods can also achieve big merit.

His words are very accurate!

I am a cultivator and shall not kill.

Sheng-yen Lu

32. Mice Squeaking

When I was living in the United States, there was a period of time I stayed in the mountain area. Let us call it, "South Mountain!" At South Mountain, there was a small community of about fifty households and most of them were Caucasians. The houses were not considered small, as every house was about six thousand square feet in size. The houses were big and each had its own architectural style. It could be considered a famous community.

When we were living there, everything was very cozy. We had sweet dreams and slept soundly. The environment was very serene and elegant; when I opened my eyes [every morning], I could see an expanse of green in the front and at the backyard. We felt carefree and relaxed, especially with the quietude of the surroundings.

Initially, I discovered a few pieces of peanut shells in my storage room for blankets. I was very astonished.

Who secretly ate peanuts here?

There was no need to suspect anyone because anyone could eat peanuts without being controlled, so there was no reason to hide in the storage room.

Who was that?

Needless to say, it must be the "mice." Especially so because mice droppings were found at the same location.

I am a cultivator and shall not kill. Initially, I did not pay any attention.

Once, while cultivating in front of the shrine, I was entering samadhi during the main section of the cultivation sadhana. The moment I closed my eyes, I heard the squeaking sound of mice. I opened my eyes and found two fluffy little things chasing [each other] between the gaps of the stair railing. The stair railing was upright, the two mice were dashing and dodging left and right in a S-shape pattern, and making squeaking sounds.

I looked at them.

Both of them looked at me without any fear. The two small green-bean eyes looked around in an unrestrained manner.

I would normally disregard this kind of performance. But they were taking advantage of a Buddhist's ethics of high tolerance, endurance, uprightness, and integrity as an opportunity of getting their way.

They intensified [their lawlessness].

They built a nest in the sofa.

The defecated and urinated everywhere.

They behaved atrociously on the dining table.

They bit through the hot gas pipe.

They played hide-and-seek in the living room even in the daytime.

They bit through clothes.

They ferociously showed fangs and claws at people.

I thought, "If I ignore the mice, they will think that they can be self-indulgent. If there is no tiger on the mountain, the monkey becomes the king. If I do not have a cat in the house, the mice would become the boss."

An American rodent control expert was called to come.

He said, "There are lots of mice in this mountain area. In the house located at the front of the mountain, I caught twenty-seven mice altogether at one time."

I asked, "Were they alive or dead?"

He said, "Poison was used, and then we found a total of twenty-seven mice in the basement."

I said, "Would it be possible to catch the mice alive and return them to other mountains?"

The rodent control expert said, "I don't know how to catch them alive, they will die if poison is used. There is one type of poison that the mice like to take. They become very thirsty after taking it, and then they need to find water to drink. They will end up dying in the river ditch."

I asked, "Is it possible to sprinkle a chemical substance that blocks them from entering?"

The expert said, "Mice are very clever, they can burrow holes in the ground to enter."

. . .

Frankly speaking, except for not being able to open the refrigerator, the mice at my home had become lawless. They considered themselves kings, wreaking havoc in my humble home; a big group of small mice also followed behind [the kings], adding to the chaos and making so much noise.

What could be done?

Suddenly, I thought of "Jambhala" (Huang Caishen, the Yellow God of Wealth). Was the hand of Huang Caishen not holding a "treasure-spouting mongoose"? He must be able to handle these "clamorous" mice.

I invocated, "*Om, jum-bah-lah, chan-lan-chah-nah-yeh, so-ha.*"

"Jambhala" put down the treasure-spouting mongoose which drove all the clown mice out of my home.

Wow! Such strong spiritual efficacy!

The treasure-spouting mongoose got rid of all the arrogant mice, and my house has no more mice!

Vajra Ucchusma is extremely ferocious. He has immeasurable dharma power and an extra-ordinary dignified appearance. His light for removing filth is inconceivable.

Sheng-yen Lu

33. Comments on Andy Lau from Head to Toe

In 2011, Andy Lau was given the best actor award in the Taipei Golden Horse Film Festival and Awards ceremony. My attention was therefore brought onto him. He started his career when he was young, and he was very popular even in his prime years. He is already fifty years old, and in the movie, television, and musical industries, he is doing well. It is very rare to have a person like this.

I comment based on his "Facial features":

Eyebrows – crescent eyebrows.

Eye – eagle eyes.

Nose – hooked eagle nose.

Mouth – fish mouth.

Ear – rabbit ears.

The Siblings Palace is on the "eyebrows." He is considered good at dealing with people, continuously cooperative, and has received lots of assistance from his benefactors.

The Sagacity Palace is on the "eyes." He is considered smart and wise, and he has the ability to perceive what is going to happen.

The Wealth Palace is on the "nose." People in general do not like to associate with people having this kind of nose because they are likely to bring harm to others. Fortunately, his eagle eyes mitigated the defects from his eagle-hooked nose. As a result, his wealth has become better.

His "Mouth," a fish mouth, is considered only average.

The Life Expectancy Palace is on the "ears." His ears are shaped like those of a rabbit, and fans out a little. His lifespan is considered average, but he has to guard against accidents.

The Emotion Palace is behind the "eyebrows." He is considered to be an affectionate person, but he is quite low-key; there are some rough patches which he will go through smoothly.

The Servant Palace is on the "chin." Andy Lau's chin is considered the worst type, for it tells of a fate that is not as good in his old age. He may lead a miserable life, and friends and relatives may desert him.

The Authority and Status Palace on the "smile lines" shows that he still has authority and status.

I was only briefly analyzing Andy Lau's facial features, the strongest parts are his "eyes" and "nose," and the worst one is his "chin."

For this type of face, he could be popular for a certain period only, yet somehow his popularity is still high when he reached fifty years old. This is an "anomaly."

This kind of face could also be that of an ordinary person, but he remains top in the entertainment performance business. This is also considered "atypical. " (He must work very hard.)

According to my observation, I classify this type of facial characteristic as "Karmic Hindrance Type." It is the type with severe karmic hindrance. Based on the "Three Pavilions":

Severe karmic hindrance.

From birth to teenager, not good. (Upper Pavilion) From hair root to eyebrow.

From teenager to prime years, not good. (Middle Pavilion) From eyebrow to nose tip. But he worked diligently and appreciated his work.

From prime years to old age, the most poor. (Lower Pavilion) From nose tip to lower chin.

These are perceived from the "three pavilions." His three pavilions of old age, middle age, and youth are all not so good. (Short and wrinkled)

It was strange that:

Currently he has reached fifty years of age, but he is still very popular. This is puzzling. According to [the above] reasoning, he should be ill-fated all along; but at fifty years old, his timing, life, and fortune, are still pretty good in the eyes of ordinary people. He is not only pretty good, but also a person at the top, standing above the clouds.

Have his karmic hindrances been purified?

I was very curious.

I thought it over and over, but still could not figure it out.

One night, God Ucchusma appeared in my dream. This Vajra is the Great Sovereign Divine King Buddha, who is manifested from Shakyamuni Buddha's heart.

He specializes in eradicating "filthy negative energy" and removing "hindrances."

Vajra Ucchusma is extremely ferocious. He has immeasurable dharma power and an extra-ordinary dignified appearance. His light for removing filth is inconceivable.

He voluntarily told me, "It is true that Andy Lau is a person originally carrying karmic hindrances, but he had endorsed the products of the toilet and bathroom fixtures manufacturer, HCG. His pictures are printed on the toilet facilities."

Vajra Ucchusma also said, "Andy Lau's merit comes from his not minding his pictures being placed on the toilets. Years of filthy negative energy eradicated all of Andy Lau's karmic hindrances, turning ominousness to auspiciousness. Once the karmic hindrances were eliminated, great fortune descended and this is the reason why Andy Lau was able to hasten fortune and avoid calamity!"

To place one's picture on the toilet long term is the "Practice of Eradicating Karmic Hindrances." This is really amazing! (Using filth to remove karmic hindrance), his high popularity could possibly continue on.

It is up to you to believe it or not!

34. Do Not Sell Fish These Few Days

I went to the western harbor fish market. The moment I stepped in, I could smell the fishy stench—which is typical of any fish market everyone knows. I came not to buy fish, but to circumambulate the giant-sized fish market one time and chant the "Deliverance Mantra."

Chanting mantra.

Forming mudra.

Visualizing.

All the souls of the fishes, prawns, and so on, were flying up; the whole space was filled with delivered spirits.

They covered the early rising red sun entirely.

I have a metaphor to describe this kind of deliverance scenario. It is like a movie, "Locusts in Transit," that I have seen before. Imagine: thousands and thousands of locusts gathering like black clouds and completely covering the big sun. This is the way I delivered the fish family.

I walked round and round.

Suddenly, a fishmonger walked in front of me and said, "Grand Master Lu, why are you here?"

I asked, "You are?"

The fishmonger replied, "I am Lianhua Fuquan, your disciple."

"Oh!" I said, as I didn't expect to encounter a disciple amongst fishmongers in the fish market.

The fishmonger said, "Grand Master Lu, you come to buy fish. I have the freshest ones and I can offer live fish to you."

I smiled and said, "I come to buy fish, but rather than buying visible fish, I want to buy invisible fish."

The fishmonger was startled, "Are there any invisible fish?"

I replied, "There are. All sentient beings have [a spirit]; how could there be none?"

I was about to leave, but the fishmonger said, "Grand Master Lu, please leave me a piece of advice."

I glanced at this fishmonger disciple, his glabella (the area between the eyebrows) was emanating blackness, I said, "Do not sell fish these few days, alright?"

The fishmonger disciple asked, "Which few days?"

I replied, "These three days."

"Are there any issues?"

"I do not know!" I replied.

The fishmonger said, "Grand Master Lu, you nevertheless have to give me a reason. I can stop selling, I will definitely listen to you. However, it will be difficult for me to explain to my family if I do not run business for three days!"

I looked at his glabella emanating blackness. Hesitantly, I said, "It is a mystery!"

"What is the mystery?"

"I do not know!"

I had a laugh and left.

I told the fishmonger disciple, "Chant the *High King Sutra* frequently to hasten auspiciousness and avoid ominousness; only then, calamities will be eradicated."

The fishmonger replied, "I will chant when I am free!"

News came later:

The fishmonger disciple did not follow my advice to stop selling fish for three days; on the second day, while lots of fish were sold, one of them was a puffer fish which a buyer brought home to cook. The whole family contracted food poisoning and was sent to the hospital for treatment.

The police traced it to the fishmonger disciple.

The fishmonger disciple argued that he "absolutely did not know it was poisonous!"

However, everyone knows that "puffer fish" are poisonous. In general, the chefs at Japanese restaurants selling "puffer fish" know how to remove the poison, but an ordinary family may not know.

He was plagued by the lawsuit that came about from the case of the "puffer fish" poisoning.

The fishmonger disciple regretted very much that he did not listen to Grand Master Lu's advice right from the outset!

I thought why not pray to the Mountain God and Earth God?

Sheng-yen Lu

35. Walking from "Wufeng" to "Dakeng"

When I was in university, I studied "Surveying." Therefore, I could read "topographic maps," and I saw that the mountains of "Wufeng" are connected with the mountains of "Dakeng."

Once, I went to the "Provincial Parliament" (at that time) of "Wufeng." Suddenly, I had a strange idea. I actually thought that I could eventually reach Dakeng just by walking from the mountain at the back of the Provincial Parliament, towards the direction to Dakeng.

I thought [I could do five things]:

First, practice mountain climbing.

Second, exercise.

Third, view feng shui.

Fourth, determine my own physical strength.

Fifth, satisfy my curiosity.

I thought, in any case, those are not high mountain ranges, for they are only a few small hills. It cannot possibly be dangerous!

I [went] alone, without carrying food or water, backpack or climbing gear. I was a surveyor before, and I had seen big mountains and small hills. These few small hills should not pose any big problem based on my robust feet work.

I thought I had very good eyesight, so as long as I walked northward, I should be able to reach "Dakeng."

Hence, since action speaks louder than words, I started walking, certain that I must be able to reach "Dakeng."

I followed a little path, and went into the mountain; at first, I could still identify the directions, and there were a few farmhouses belonging to the mountain residents. I felt reassured since there were people living here.

I therefore walked over a hill.

And over another hill.

And over another hill again.

At this time, I felt something was not quite right.

Those little paths that were trekked out by people became tinier and tinier. Eventually, they became tiny trails. (Trails mean little path.)

After crossing over three small hills, I felt a bit out of breath.

I felt extremely thirsty.

Having only crossed over three hills, I looked around from the top of the hill—front, back, left, and right—and found that the hills were joined one after the other continuously with no end. They were the same all around.

I walked from the human-cultivated dryland in the mountain to the uncultivated valley.

Startlingly I realized:

I completely lost my sense of direction—east, south, west, and north.

Physical strength was sapping.

The surrounding environment had been changed, I was trapped in the valley.

Mountains were in all directions, and I did not know which mountain was the one leading to "Dakeng."

If I continued walking forward regardless of the situation, would I be going deeper and deeper into the mountain?

My mind became blank.

I felt extremely frightened.

Once this kind of feeling sprung up, fear set in, and my field of vision was filled with just an expanse of forest. I cried out miserably! Although I was bold and skillful, yet this time, I admit that I could not possibly return home.

I was afraid to venture forward!

But which direction would bring me back to the Provincial Parliament? I was already at the point of "having roamed over all the mountains and streams and suspected there was no way out," and where will there be "another village where the willow trees give shade and the flowers bloom light"? [Meaning I was already in the situation where there was no way out and I was looking for the light at the end of the tunnel?]

I thought why not pray to the Mountain God and Earth God?

I recited the Local Earth Deity Mantra:

"*Namo, san-man-duo, mu-tuo-nan, om, du-lu-du-lu, di-wei, so-ha.*" Three times.

My left leg stamped three times on the ground.

Oh no! There was no response at all. I was destined to die in the mountains.

Suddenly, I became aware that far away behind me was a big tree, and it seemed there was a person under the tree. I moved my body closer to the big tree, and an old man was really sitting under the tree smoking. He had bronze-colored skin; his upper body was naked and he was wearing a pair of black shorts.

I asked, "What is the way back to the Provincial Parliament?"

The old man replied, "To the right walk straight, you will see a small path. Follow that path and walk around the mountain for one and a half hours. You will return to the Provincial Parliament."

I felt ecstatic, walked a couple steps, and wanted to turn back round to thank the old man. When I turned back, where was that old man? Only two, three seconds, and the old man disappeared. Oh Heavens! Mountain God, Earth God, gods and spirits manifested!

I finally returned to level ground! Thanks to Heaven and Earth!

36. Truly Seeing

Ever since the initiation of my divine eyes, the number of buddhas and bodhisattvas that I have seen are innumerable. In particular, on the day when my divine eyes were initiated, from the "Four Enlightened [Realms]" to the "Six Non-enlightened [Realms]," I traveled the whole ten dharma realms once. Heavens! So it is actually like this, so it is actually like this.

I called myself "Padmakumara," the reason of which comes from the fact that I had truly seen "Padmakumara."

This was the basis on which I wrote two hundred and twenty-six books. If I, Grand Master Lu, utter any false words, then may the Taiwanese expression apply to me: "Yaoshou!" [It means, "Premature death."]

Certainly, not only did I just see Padmakumara, but during samadhi, I also truly saw.

Is it an "illusion"? I say no.

Is it "self-deception"? I say no.

Is it a "shadow"? I say no.

Is it a "misperception"? I say no.

Is it an "abnormality"? I say no.

Is it a "crazy thought"? I say no.
Is it a "random thought"? I say no.
Am I "dreaming"? I say no.
I can only say, my seeing, is true seeing.
Here are several small examples!

First:
I was in Mainland China, and on the plane from Beijing to Taiyuan. During samadhi, I truly saw "Western Paradise Amitabha Buddha." Words could hardly describe his "Hugeness," "Magnificence," and "Brilliance."
It was extremely inconceivable!
In particular, his feet, which were stepping on the lotus flower, were extremely exquisite.
Amitabha Buddha said, "For every action, uphold the precepts, and one will then have peace."

Second:
I was in Gyeongju City of South Korea to pay my respects to Medicine Vaidurya Light King Buddha. I performed the great homage with full-body prostrations.
On my return trip in the car, during samadhi, I truly saw Medicine Vaidurya Light King Buddha, Bhaisajyaraja Bodhisattva (Medicine King Bodhisattva), Bhaisajyasamudgata Bodhisattva (Medicine Superior Bodhisattva), Sunlight Bodhisattva, Moonlight Bodhisattva, and The Twelve Divine Generals of Medicine Buddha.
Every venerable revealed an incomparably dignified golden body.
With ten thousand rays of radiant light.
A thousand strobes of auspicious energies.
Medicine Vaidurya Light King Buddha said, "Your sickness will be cured!"
At that time, I had the "four great dispersions," and the "skull-

splitting-into-eight-petals" phenomenon. I fully recovered later on. It really was a miracle.

Third:

I was in Taiwan.

At that time, I had just encountered a matter that I was dragged into without any reason, it seemed there was no way out, with lots of difficulties.

During samadhi, I truly saw Namo Avalokitesvara Bodhisattva, who opened up a smile on her face.

The bodhisattva's golden body and brightness, were so beautiful that nothing could describe it, surpassing everyone ever seen before, and no one could compare with her beauty.

Avalokitesvara Bodhisattva said to me, "Every matter has been resolved!"

It was on the same day that I saw the bodhisattva, the news came to us that everything had been resolved.

Fourth:

I was in Seattle in the United States.

On the first day, while expounding *The Great Exposition of Secret Mantra*, during samadhi, I truly saw Lineage Master Tsongkhapa, Lineage Master of the Yellow Sect in Tibetan Buddhism (Gelugpa), appear in the space right above the front of my seat.

Lineage Master Tsongkhapa radiated brilliance that continuously blessed me softly and gently. This kind of brightness was indescribable.

Secret.

Soft.

Delicate.

Energetic.

Lineage Master Tsongkhapa said to me, "Blessing Grand Master Lu for expounding *The Great Exposition of Secret Mantra*!"

(I gave these four small examples to showcase the very truth of the truth. After I attained the path of seeing, awakened and achieved enlightenment, I understood the arising and cessation of phenomena and the arising and cessation of the mind. Everything I understood thoroughly.)

37. Do Not Cling to the Inexistence of "Padmakumara"

In Mainland China, at Lanzhou University, there was detailed research on the caves of Dunhuang, and a book was written, *The Dunhuang Story of Buddhism*, which mentioned Padmakumara. It described two Padmakumaras in the time period of Golden Light Buddha, and the process by which they cultivated to become Bodhisattvas. One of the Padmakumaras was Avalokitesvara Bodhisattva, and the other Padmakumara was Mahasthamaprapta Bodhisattva.

If you were to go to Dunhuang and ask the administrator, "Which cave has Padmakumara inside?"

The administrator would answer, "Every cave has Padmakumara."

If you were to ask, "Within Cave No. 314, are all Padmakumara?"

The administrator would answer, "Yes."

In Taiwan, Zhang Mingcong, who is interested in researching on the history of Buddhism, presented more evidence.

He listed various Padmakumaras, complete with pictures and narratives. He said, "There are uncountable Padmakumaras."

I often explain like this:

The *Amitabha Sutra* states, "In the west, there are ten trillion Buddha-lands. Amongst these, there is a Buddha named Amitabha."

Let us think about it:

Ten trillion Buddha-lands.

That is ten trillion Buddha fields (Pure Lands).

For every Buddha-land there is a dwelling Buddha. Do you know the epithets of the Buddhas in the ten trillion Buddha-lands?

In *High King Sutra*:

Fifteen hundred Buddhas – what are their epithets?

Fifteen thousand Buddhas – what are their epithets?

All the countless Buddhas – what are their epithets?

Can Buddhist disciples count all the buddha epithets in the buddha pure lands?

And:

Still again, for people who cling on to the eighth consciousness, "Tathagatagarbha Consciousness" (Alaya Consciousness), the six sutras of the Consciousness-only school of Buddhism are as follows:

Samdhinirmocana Sutra.

Avatamsaka Sutra.

Lankavatara Sutra.

Ghanavyuha Sutra (*Houyan Sutra*).

Mahayana-Abhidharma Sutra.

Sutra of the Appearance of the Thus Come One (*Ru Lai Chu Xian Gong De Jing*).

(The above are the Six Sutras of Consciousness-only.)

In fact, in the research on the Consciousness-only school, various knowledgeable teachers of Buddhist studies, have many different ways of connoting Consciousness-only:

One consciousness connotation – of the Satyasiddhi Sect.

Two consciousnesses connotation – in the Awakening of Faith in the Mahayana.

Three consciousnesses connotation – in the *Lankavatara Sutra.*

Five consciousnesses connotation – in the Awakening of Faith in the Mahayana.

Six consciousnesses connotation – in the *Abhidharma Mahavibhasa Sastra, Abhidharmakosa Sastra, Treatise on the Ability to Quantify* (*Nengliang Lun*), *Pramanavarttika.*

Eight consciousnesses connotation – of the Consciousness-only Sect (Yogacara School).

Nine consciousnesses connotation – in the *Mahayana-samgraha-sastra.*

Ten consciousnesses connotation – in the *Moheyan Lun* (*Commentary on the Awakening of Faith*).

Eleven consciousnesses connotation – in *Vasubandhu's Commentary on the Mahayana-samgraha-sastra* (*Vasubandhu's Mahayanasamgraha-bhasya*).

(There is even the connotation of [one mind is] limitless consciousness, in the *Garbhadhatu Treatise of Eastern Esoteric Buddhism.*)

(Void Consciousness connotation – in Sheng-yen Lu's Treatise.)

I personally feel that the eighty-four thousand teachings of the Tathagata are for treating the eighty-four thousand afflictions of sentient beings. They are completely not cast in stone to adhere to one rigid format; it is all about prescribing the right medicine for a specific illness. Hence, the right teaching at the right time reflects the unobstructed and great expedient wisdom of Buddhism. It is also wrong to only understand and cling to "the Eighth Consciousness." Mahayana Buddhism is fundamentally an immeasurable expedient means that is unobstructed and non-self.

Someone asked Reverend Zhaozhou, "What is Zhaozhou?"

Reverend Zhaozhou replied, "East gate, west gate, south gate, north gate." (That really means no obstruction, no-self, immeasurableness, and no attachment.)

I personally have witnessed Padmakumara and Lotus Light Unhindered Buddha [a.k.a. Lotus Light Self-Mastery Buddha]. If you say they do not exist, that means you still have not personally witnessed and confirmed [their existence]. If you have witnessed and confirmed it yourself, then you will know this is not false.

If you only know that the "well" exists but do not know the existence of the "big sea," it is a pity!

38. Do Not Go to the Seaside!

One year, a disciple by the surname Tao, brought his wife to see me.

Disciple Tao ran a construction business and was quite well-known. He was a devoted disciple.

Every time he came to see me, he always brought some souvenirs such as grape wines, biscuits, or local specialties. On the one hand, they were for offering to Grand Master Lu, and on the other hand, they were for offering to all the venerables on the shrine. He never came empty-handed.

Disciple Tao always asked for some tips for cultivation, for example:

"What is the sensation when the expedient energy (qi) is converted to wisdom energy (qi)?"

"What is the pith instruction for the energy (qi) of left and right channels entering into the central channel?"

"What is the pith instruction for descending and spreading the light drops?"

I would briefly and concisely tell disciple Tao the pith instructions and the main points.

This time, disciple Tao also brought his wife. Disciple Tao's wife was very young. She had no religious belief, was an atheist, and her beauty was that of glamor.

Every time disciple Tao attended ceremonies, he was always alone by himself.

(It was because his wife had no interest.)

This time she came along because disciple Tao had persuaded her several times, and she then reluctantly agreed.

She was dressed head-to-toe in name brand clothing. She faced the shrine, but did not even want to put her palms together.

When she saw disciple Tao pay homage to me with full-body prostrations, she displayed a bit of disdain.

Disciple Tao discussed buddhadharma with me, but she was indifferent and her expression was stiff.

She only watched the cars on the street outside that were speeding in both directions. She returned to her seat and gazed at me to size me up for a while.

She felt bored, and looked at the "Chopard" watch on her hand.

When disciple Tao was about to leave, she suddenly asked me, "I heard people say that your divination is very accurate, is that true or not?"

"There are always rumors," I said.

"Can you look at my fate?"

"Very good."

"Is there anything I need to be concerned with?" She asked.

I stabilized my mind for a moment; once my eyes closed, I saw "Poseidon," the sea god in Greek mythology.

I was quite astonished.

I said to Mrs. Tao, "Do not go to the seaside!"

Mrs. Tao replied to me, "Do not worry! I do not know how to swim, and do not go to the beach to swim. When traveling abroad, any water activities such as motorized water sports, water skiing, scuba diving, glass-bottom boating, parasailing, or banana boating...."

I would never take part in.

"Even at high-class clubs, I would only wear the swimsuit and sun-tan at the side of the swimming pool. I won't actually enter the water. I have no affinity with water."

Mrs. Tao then said, "Grand Master Lu, did you miscalculate?"

I replied, "Perhaps!"

But, I still advised her, "Do not go to the seaside!"

Disciple Tao together with his wife, drove away in his luxurious car.

One year later, Mrs. Tao forgot the words that I told her.

Once, she followed a tour to a scenic district of a certain country. Everyone was standing on the rocks along the seaside to take pictures. That day, strong gusty winds of level eleven bellowed.

Mrs. Tao wanted to have a picture by herself.

A piece of high reef was chosen.

The ocean spray shot up from behind and exploded just like fireworks. Mrs. Tao had her back towards the sea to have her picture taken.

A strong gusty wind swept across.

The waves became huge.

All of a sudden, a big wave rolled in and receded, and Mrs. Tao was drawn into the sea. In only an instant, her body was not seen floating up. Her body had already sunk to the bottom of the sea.

No amount of dredging could find her!

Oh Heavens! Disciple Tao cried his eyes out, and requested me to perform a bardo deliverance for her.

Disciple Tao told me, "She had forgotten Grand Master Lu's warning of 'do not go to the seaside!'"

The great teacher of the universal consciousness, able to carry out the path of loving-kindness; able to carry out the path of loving-kindness, able to carry out the path of great loving-kindness; the one who is able to carry out the path of loving-kindness of the Shakya clan, auspiciousness and perfection.

Sheng-yen Lu

39. One Scene from "Bowl of Rice Cake Shop (Dian Kou Wan Guo)"

At the end of November 2011, in an entourage of disciples that included Master Lianning, Master Liandian, Lianya, and Lianzeng, we ate rice cakes at the "Bowl of Rice Cake Shop" in the neighborhood of the National Taiwan Museum of Fine Arts in Taichung. The rice cakes of this Bowl of Rice Cake Shop were very popular, and every afternoon, it would always be packed with people. Most of the time, people had to make reservations before coming to have the rice cake!

Hung on the wall of the Bowl of Rice Cake Shop were a painting and a calligraphy couplet that I admired. The painting in the center was Samantabhadra Bodhisattva riding on an elephant. The couplet, with one verse on each side of the painting, was written by the calligrapher, Lu Foting.

The second verse of the couplet read, "Able in loving-kindness is my master."

I asked, "Who is the Able in loving-kindness?"

Lianning, Liandian, Lianya, Liandeng, and the rest, looked at one another, speechless.

I said, "Able in loving-kindness is Shakyamuni Buddha."

I explained:

We chant the mantra of Shakyamuni Buddha:

"*Om, mou-ni, mou-ni, ma-ha-mou-ni, shi-jia-mou-ni, so-ha.*"

"Mou-ni" in this mantra represents "Able in loving-kindness."

The explanation of the mantra is as follows:

"The great teacher of the universal consciousness, able to carry out the path of loving-kindness; able to carry out the path of loving-kindness, able to carry out the path of great loving-kindness; the one who is able to carry out the path of loving-kindness of the Shakya clan, auspiciousness and perfection."

Therefore I said, "Able in loving-kindness is Shakyamuni Buddha."

While I was explaining, two ladies came in through the entrance of the shop. Both of them waved at me, and said, "We are your disciples!"

One of the disciples said, "About several months ago, we met while Grand Master Lu and fellow disciples were eating rice cakes at 'Bowl of Rice Cake Shop.' I kneeled down and prayed for Grand Master's blessing. It was because I had been married for eleven years, but I could not get pregnant. I had seen lots of famous doctors of Traditional Chinese and Western medicines, but the results were still negative. Knowing that Grand Master Lu has great dharma power, I therefore prayed for great blessing."

The disciple continued saying, "At that time, Grand Master Lu stood up to bless me on the head. Through Grand Master's palm on my top of my head, I could feel the dharma stream coursing down my whole body continuously without stopping, there was an expanse of brightness in front of my eyes. Subsequently, after I went home, I became pregnant. I am truly thankful to Grand Master Lu. Now, I am praying for a safe delivery for me and my child."

I finally remembered:

This lady disciple, several months ago, had kneeled in front of me, praying for "pregnancy" blessing.

The reason was, she had been married for eleven years but was infertile.

I closed my eyes, and saw the Samantabhadra Bodhisattva on the wall radiate light which entered into the womb of the lady disciple.

Wow! The response in my hand was very strong. That kind of vibration power was generated from the union of the Bodhisattva with my hand.

Inside the light that entered into the womb of the lady disciple, there was a small child.

At last, a few months later.

She was pregnant!

I told the lady disciple, "This child will be a great sage in the future!"

Everyone in the Bowl of Rice Cake Shop saw this scene.

And:

There was a disciple who lived very far away overseas; she had been infertile for twenty years.

Twenty years, plus twenty years [of age] before marriage—she was already forty years of age; would it be possible for her to give birth?

She did not give up. She prayed to the Padmakumara statue and prepared the greatest offerings.

That night, she saw Padmakumara dressed in white robe, extraordinarily dignified, and wearing a Five Buddha Crown. There were five colors of precious jewels on the crown. Amongst them, a red precious jewel fell onto the hand of Padmakumara that immediately transformed into an exquisite cute little baby.

Padmakumara said to the lady disciple, "This baby is given to you!"

In her dream, her belly became large. When she woke up, she told her husband that she had a baby in her belly.

Her husband replied, "Thoughts in the daytime may get reflected in dreams at night. How can dreams be accurate?"

But, since that day, the lady disciple really became pregnant.

Now, her parents-in-law all took refuge, and so did her relatives and friends. Many people took refuge. All just because one dream led to a pregnancy!

40. I Will Take You to Fly

On Saturday, December 10, 2011, I was in Taiwan Lei Zang Temple presiding over the "Treasure Source Tara" homa ceremony. On that day, over ten thousand people attended and listened to my exposition of the origination of Treasure Source Tara.

After the dharma talk, I also bestowed the empowerment of "Treasure Source Tara" to the crowd. During the empowerment, I had a special sensation.

Treasure Source Tara appeared in gold from the space; her appearance was similar to "Green Tara." She flew freely above the empowerment banner and her flying postures were not like a flying bird, but rather in various standing or sitting postures. One hand formed the wish-granting mudra and the other hand was holding an "Utpala flower." Different kinds of light emanated from her ten finger tips and the Utpala flower.

Within the lights were lots of treasures:

Lotus flowers.

Jeweled carts.

Golden lamps.

Auspicious fruits.

Incense oils (Vilepana).
Dharma wheels.
Water with eight merits.
Fragrant flowers.
Buddha-fruit.
Sublime bliss.
Flying shoes.
Etc…

Limitless seven treasures, eight treasures, twenty-one treasures, thirty-two treasures, and thirty-seven treasures, continuously descended from the space onto all disciples; even I, Living Buddha Sheng-yen Lu, also received one treasure, "Flying shoes." I picked them up, and kept them close to my chest.

Treasure Source Tara asked me, "Grand Master Lu, you already can fly, what is the benefit of having the flying shoes?"

I replied, "I will bring someone with me to fly."

Treasure Source Tara asked, "Fly to where?"

I replied, "Fly to the pure land of Maha Twin Lotus Ponds."

Treasure Source Tara said, "Why not fly to the pure land of Samantabhadra Buddha Mother, which is the origin of Treasure Source Tara."

I answered, "Buddha pure lands are all interconnected, I certainly will make offerings to the pure land of Samantabhadra Buddha Mother."

Treasure Source Tara said, "Excellent! Excellent!"

After the ceremony, a disciple asked me, "Grand Master Lu, I heard that you could spiritually travel to the Buddha worlds of the ten directions, right?"

I replied, "I can fly."

Disciple asked, "Can you take me to fly?"

I suddenly remembered that in my chest I had the "flying shoes" bestowed by Treasure Source Tara. I thought, what a coincidence that

41. Cao Cangming Thus Said

On December 10, 2011, after the "Treasure Source Tara" homa (fire offering) ceremony was completed at around six o'clock in the evening, I went to have my dinner at the dining hall of Taiwan Lei Zang Temple.

A Mr. Cao Cangming was sitting next to me, at my right.

He said, "I knew Grand Master Lu over thirty years ago."

I was startled. I asked, "How old were you at that time?"

He answered, "At that time, I was studying primary school." (Dharma brother was now over forty years old.)

I asked, "How did you know me while studying primary school?"

He answered, "My mother brought me to see you to ask about my father. The location was at Jinhua Road. I felt that Grand Master Lu could really tell jokes. When adults listened to you, they laughed heartily!"

He said, "During that time, my father, who was serving at the police force, was the head of the local police station near Deji Reservoir. He and Grand Master Lu's father, Lu Ershun, had frequent contact with each other. My father frequently chatted with Grand Master's father. They were very close. And also because of this, my father and mother were able to visit Grand Master Lu."

He said, "Grand Master Lu's divination is really accurate!"

I asked, "How accurate is it?"

He answered, "My father was investigating a criminal case, and came seeking Grand Master Lu for instructions. Grand Master Lu had said, at a certain time and month, he would be able to capture this criminal by going to Yanchao Township in Kaohsiung City."

"The result?"

He said, "The result was, he really caught the criminal! Due to this achievement, my father was transferred from Taichung County to Taichung City. Eventually, my father became a Senior Inspector and he remained so until he retired."

He also said, "Grand Master Lu's divination for my uncle is the most accurate."

"How so?"

He said, "Grand Master Lu asserted that my uncle could become the Chief Inspector in the police force, and my uncle really did become the Chief Inspector. Grandmaster also told my uncle to be careful at fifty years old."

"The result?"

He said, "At age fifty, he unexpectedly died of a heart attack!"

I asked, "I did not say that he would die, did I?"

He said, "You did not. Grand Master Lu only said, to be careful at age fifty."

He also said, "When my uncle became Chief Inspector, and died at age fifty of a heart attack, it was considered quite sensational. The news media even published it."

Cao Cangming said, "At that time, Grand Master Lu was at Taichung giving consultations. It created quite a stir. You were surrounded by many people everyday. My whole family came to ask Grand Master Lu for guidance—my father, mother, aunt, and uncle. The most accurate was the capture of the criminal, and the death of my uncle at age fifty.

Even the time, place, and age, was without deviation."

I asked, "Has your father ever come to Taiwan Lei Zang Temple?"

"He came before. He had always wanted to acknowledge the old relationship with Grand Master Lu's father. It was just that your father, maybe, had forgotten him. When he knew old Mr. Lu Ershun had passed away, my father, in those days, was grief-stricken. He was continuously silent and not speaking!"

"Alas! Time passes really quickly! Hard to imagine that I am already sixty-seven years old, and you are also over forty. When I was giving consultation, I was only over twenty years old, and you were only in primary school."

There is one saying:

"Human life is a live broadcast. Furthermore, there are no NGs"

Buddhadharma does not part from secular dharma. This is how it is!

Sheng-yen Lu

42. "Lotus Leaf Child" Sadhana

There was once a Buddhist layperson who enjoyed a great reputation in the Buddhist community. He knew both Vajrayana and Sutrayana very well. This great layperson was also a rich and powerful person. He donated money to build temples, to print sutras, to offer to the Sangha, and to do good deeds. In the religious community, everyone knew about him.

When he was living abroad in New York, he printed a sutra. Very few people know about this sutra. It was not widely circulated. The sutra is called *Lotus Leaf Child Sutra*. I came across this sutra by accident.

In the sutra, it teaches people that offering to the "Lotus Leaf Child" has great benefits:

1. Increase in fortune.
2. Improvement in wisdom.
3. Great power and prestige.
4. Great supernatural powers.
5. Extension of life.

The statue of "Lotus Leaf Child" can be made using wood, porcelain, glass, clay, or stone. A model of a child standing on a lotus leaf is molded; the hair is tied into two buns on top of the head. The child can be male or female.

One head, two arms. The two hands, each extending an index finger. One finger pointing at the earth, the other pointing to the heavens.

(Similar to the child statue of Shakyamuni Buddha of the Buddha Bathing Festival.)

The difference between this statue and that of the child statue of Shakyamuni Buddha is the standing on the lotus leaf and also the two hair buns on top of the head.

The offering sadhana in the sutra is:

Offering is to be done in a private room.

(Chickens, dogs, cats, and the like, are not allowed to enter.)

Offerings are flowers, incense, light, tea, fruits, children's toys, and candies, etc.

Incense is to be lit three times a day: morning, noon, and night.

Cultivation practice is to be done in the afternoon.

Visualize "Lotus Leaf Child."

Chant: (Mudra: one hand pointing to the heaven, one hand pointing to the earth.)

"*Heaven Spirit, Earth Spirit, Lotus Leaf Child Spirit. Ji-ji-lu-ling. Seh.*"

(The more the better)

Entering of the Principal Deity into Oneself (*Ru-wo*) and Release of Oneself into the Cosmic Consciousness (*Wo-ru*).

(Similar to entering samadhi.)

The above is the essential part of the sadhana. The others like paying homage, making offerings, making wishes, etc., are done according to one's abilities.

In this way, it can be done once a day or three times a day, depending on each person's preference, but it should not be interrupted.

One needs to chant until "Lotus Leaf Child" appears in one's own dream before it is then considered to be "yogic response."

The pith instructions:

The cultivator has to eat the offerings.

If the offerings have spoiled, it should be discarded and changed to fresh ones.

The essence:

Sincerity.

Dedication.

After yogic union, "Lotus Leaf Child" will stand by you like a shadow. If the cultivator were to pray to Lotus Leaf Child for wealth, wealth will then come; if one were to pray for fame and status, fame and status then follows; if one were to pray for children, children will then come; if one were to pray for a boyfriend or girlfriend, a boyfriend or girlfriend will then come; if one were to pray for marriage, marriage will then come; if one were to pray for an exam, the performance on the exam will be good; if one were to pray for food and drink, food and drink will follow.

After yogic union, if one were to pray for wisdom of the Buddha, one will have clear understanding when reading scriptures; if one were to pray for various deities, various deities will appear; if one were to pray for wisdom to grow, wisdom will then grow; if one were to pray for supernatural powers, supernatural powers will also appear.

After yogic union, Lotus Leaf Child can "respond to you in a dream," that is, he will inform about auspiciousness, ominousness, calamity, fortune, and so on.

Grand Master Lu hereto tells everyone, the "Lotus Leaf Child" Sadhana is similar to the "Child Reporting to the Ear" Practice, but it is a bit more superior.

The "Lotus Leaf Child," I categorize him in a list of "gods" that everyone can pray to and worship.

A Buddhist, of course, does not have to cultivate the "Lotus Leaf Child" Practice.

But, if they have the supernormal powers of "Lotus Leaf Child," it would certainly be an assisting force to learning Buddhism.

There are indeed buddhas and bodhisattvas.

There are indeed various gods of all heavens.

There are indeed dakinis.

There is indeed "Lotus Leaf Child."

This is truly present in the secular world. Buddhadharma does not part from secular dharma. This is how it is!

43. Letting You Know Through Your "Dream"

One True Buddha School disciple, "Lianhua Changyu," who was about fifty years old, and his wife, Mrs. Chen Ting, were invited to participate in a pilgrimage group of a nearby temple. They travel to an ancestral shrine for their pilgrimage.

The pilgrimage is a popular custom in Taiwan. For instance, every year, the Goddess Mazu is lifted in a sedan chair at Zhenlan Palace in Dajia to Fengtian Palace in Xingang.

This temple event can be considered number one in the whole province. They are number one in having the most people, welcoming Mazu, receiving Mazu, participating in the procession, burning incense, etc...

In Dajia's Mazu Parade, besides Mazu, there are still Qian Li Yan (the General of Thousand Mile Sight), Shun Feng Er (the General of Brilliant Hearing), and various deities following. The leaders of the parade are quite many.

Central senior officials, regional senior officials, and a very large number of worshippers, stir up a commotion along the way. It can be said that this is a very grand occasion for the entire country.

This Mazu Mania of Taiwan during the third lunar month is not a small affair.

As for:

It goes without saying that there are so many temples of all sizes in the whole province of Taiwan, as well as deities, that it is practically impossible to count them all.

With the buses of the pilgrimage groups going here and there, tides of people going to the temple event, and the Ba Jia Jiang (bodyguards and attendants), Taiwan has become a believer of a diverse array of religious customs.

The pilgrimage group that "Lianhua Changyu" and his wife participated in was scheduled to start their journey.

On the night before they were to start their journey, they each had a dream.

Grand Master Lu appeared in their dream, and told them, "Do not go tomorrow!"

"Why?"

"There will be a motor vehicle accident!"

"In the vehicle are statues of Third Prince, Mazu, City God, Wang Ye, etc... Many deities are on the vehicle protecting it. There should not be anything happening."

Grand Master Lu said, "The calamity is inevitable!"

The husband and wife saw Grand Master Lu's warning in their dream at the same time. As a result, they were hesitating and could not decide on whether or not to go.

However, Lianhua Changyu was one of the group leaders, and also one of the leaders of the vicinity. If the leader were to play truant, how was he going to explain; the pilgrimage group was also suggested by the vicinity's elders. If they do not go, they would be letting down these elders.

Cancelling was also not possible.

They could only summon up courage and participate. They were thinking that it was only a dream and dreams were not necessarily real.

At the end, their only solution was to wear a "Padmakumara" protection amulet on their bodies. The pilgrimage group set off as planned.

The whole bus journey went without a hitch. There were altogether three buses following one another. Lianhua Changyu was originally riding on the first bus, but was later switched to ride on the second bus. The pilgrimage also went very smoothly.

On their return journey, at Alishan, while they were on the turning point at the mid-height of the mountain, the brakes of the first bus suddenly failed.

As a result, the bus crashed against the road barrier and overturned. The impact caused it to dash out towards the slope. The car laid on its side at the roadside.

Heavens! It really was a motor vehicle accident!

The police and ambulance all arrived!

Of the worshippers on the bus, one person died and seventeen people suffered severe injuries. They were admitted to the local hospital.

Finally--

Lianhua Changyu said:

He was supposed to ride on the first bus. On the return trip, he boarded the first bus, and found that his seat was already taken by another person. The person sitting there had said, "No need to change seats, just sit in my seat on the second bus." Subsequently, Lianhua Changyu and even his wife, were then allocated to the second bus.

The problem was, the person who had switched seats with Lianhua Changyu, was the very one person who died in the motor vehicle accident.

Heavens, how could this be?

Had Lianhua Changyu not switched seats, would he be the one who died?

Was it fate?

Was it coincidence?

Was it the effect of the protection amulet?

Lianhua Changyu said, “When the pilgrimage group was on the road on Alishan, while spiraling downwards, we smelled waves of incense fragrance. Was it Padmakumara protecting? But, why did he not protect the people on the first bus?”

44. The Significance of Mo-Ding Blessing

While I am in Taiwan, every Saturday at three in the afternoon, at Taiwan Lei Zang Temple of Tiger Mountain in the middle of Caotun Town, there is a gathering of about ten thousand worshipping disciples.

They take part in the "homa" fire offering that I conduct.

They respectfully listen to me expound the *Platform Sutra of the Sixth Patriarch* and others.

They receive the empowerments of various deities.

(The banner canopy empowerments of various deities.)

After dinner time, they spontaneously line up in two rows, the majority kneeling. When I get to the middle of the crowd, I give them blessing by mo-ding one by one.

From my mouth, I recite the dharani. In my mind, I am the personal deity. I serve to bestow blessing to sentient beings.

Eliminate sickness, please!

Increase good fortune, please!

Enhance wisdom, please!

Perfect love and respect, please!

Make debtors and enemies go away, please!

Happiness and bliss, please!

No disasters and hardships, please!

Etc, etc, etc…

This "mo-ding blessing" of mine takes about one hour. With singular focus, I give all the disciples mo-ding blessing.

"The power of lineage blessing," "the power of the personal deity," "the power of the guru," "the power of the dharma protector," "the power of the mind," "the power of the mantra," all kinds of power are combined and poured into the bodies and minds of the disciples and believers.

Many miracles have resulted:

The blind can see!

The deaf can hear!

Sickness disappears!

Business becomes good!

Exams are passed!

The family is harmonious!

Wealth and promotion are gained!

Disaster and calamity disperse!

Wishes are fulfilled!

Etc, etc, etc…

Grand Master Lu believes that I have this kind of ability, only because the source of my blessing power is unending. I truly know that my lineage power is real and not false. My personal deity has yogic union with me; the personal deity's power is real and not false. My dharma protector is always by my side; my dharma protector's power is real and not false.

My thoughts are: to give to sentient beings.

I give my mantra power to sentient beings.

There was once a disciple who asked me to help him consecrate his shrine that he put up and arranged on his own.

I promised.

But I was truly too busy.

Every time I give mo-ding blessing to disciples and believers, this disciple would be kneeling among the crowd.

When I approached him, he raised his head to look at me and said, "Please consecrate my shrine!"

I answered, "Ok!"

I took some "rice" and scattered a few grains on his head, and then on the photograph of his shrine held in his hands.

I said, "I have already consecrated it for you!"

When he returned home, he surprisingly discovered that his shrine at home was already scattered with rice. This rice was on the shrine and also on the ground. It was really inconceivable. No one scattered rice on the shrine, but rice was all over it.

He said, "Grand Master Lu's supernatural power is too inconceivable. My shrine was automatically consecrated!"

(The Vajrayana method of consecration requires the scattering of rice.)

Also:

After receiving mo-ding blessing, there are those whose cancer tumors automatically disappear, and there are many! [The news] spreads from one to ten, from ten to one hundred, from one hundred to ten million. Everyone comes to ask for mo-ding blessing!

There was one little girl in a wheelchair who had gone through many mo-ding blessings. Now unexpectedly, she can stand up.

When I was at "Gan Lu Ching Tze Temple" presiding over the "Flaming Mouth" ceremony, she stood up and again asked me to give her mo-ding blessing!

These death-row convicts only took refuge in Grand Master Lu, paid Great Homage to his picture, and chanted: "*Om, gu-ru, lian-sheng, sid-dhi, hum.*"

Sheng-yen Lu

45. All Will Have Sariras

After my father, Lu Ershun, passed away, his body was delivered to "Shui Li" to be cremated. Cremation revealed sariras and sarira flowers.

The people who were present at that time included many masters, reverends, senior reverends, chapter chairpersons, dharma instructors, dharma assistants, fellow disciples, etc…

Everyone was amazed at what he or she saw.

These sariras and sarira flowers were very carefully selected and collected by Reverend Lianqin.

During his lifetime, my father, Lu Ershun, did not believe in any religion. He also did not chant the Buddha's name or diligently cultivate Vajrayana.

My father frequently said to me, "Once dead! There is nothing left!"

He did not believe in the existence of heaven, and did not believe in the existence of hell.

He once said to someone, "Because my son believes in the Buddha, studies Buddhism, and also propagates the dharma to save sentient beings, I talk very little [about the subject]. I do not want to oppose my son."

In his later years, my father changed a little. When I was propagating the dharma to a crowd, he would come to listen, and also accepted empowerments.

When I asked him to chant "*Namo Guan Shi Yin Pu Sa*," he was willing to chant "*Namo Guan Shi Yin Pu Sa*."

He also accepted my blessing and mo-ding.

In this way--

"My father also had sariras and sarira flowers."

It is really a miracle.

Also:

Quite a long time ago, in Singapore's Changi Prison, many convicts who were sentenced to death were locked up. There were convicts who had heard of my name.

Therefore, the death-row convicts took refuge in me one after another.

They just took a small picture of me and stuck it on the prison cell wall.

They paid homage to the picture.

They chanted:

"*Om, gu-ru, lian-sheng, sid-dhi, hum.*"

The sounds of the mantra reverberated continuously in the prison.

It was said that the prisoners chanted so much that the wall emitted light.

Many death-row convicts saw Grand Master Lu appear in their dreams. They were extremely excited.

After they were hung and cremated, plump sariras were rolling around on the ground. The sariras arranged themselves like a *bagua* [eight trigrams or symbols used in Taoist cosmology], from large to small, forming a large circle.

Sariras from death-row convicts.

A worldwide sensation.

These death-row convicts only took refuge in Grand Master Lu, paid Great Homage to his picture, and chanted: "*Om, gu-ru, lian-sheng, sid-dhi, hum.*"

Just like this…

Each and every one had sariras after cremation.

Also:

A born-handicapped, wheelchair-bound little girl suffering from multiple organ degeneration had heard of Grand Master's name.

Approaching death, she requested to take refuge.

She recited, "*Om, gu-ru, lian-sheng, sid-dhi, hum.*"

After she died, upon cremation, five-colored sariras and sarira flowers were found [in the ashes].

Her family members were very astonished.

They asked me, "Is this for real?"

I replied, "It is real."

Her family members asked, "Sitting in a wheelchair, she could not form mudras and did not know how to cultivate. She only wholeheartedly wanted to take refuge, and just before her death, she continuously recited the Guru Mantra. There were surprisingly five-colored sariras and sarira flowers obtained in this way. It is unbelievable!"

I answered, "Singular staunch faith, that is enough!"

I honestly tell everyone, if one wholeheartedly pays respect to Root Lineage Guru Living Buddha Lian-sheng Sheng-yen Lu, prostrates, makes offerings, recites mantras, and prays, the power generated is inconceivable. After death, one can be reborn [in paradise] and have sariras and sarira flowers. It is amazing. These are all entirely true.

To acknowledge and correct one's actions, thereupon, is the greatest blessing!

Sheng-yen Lu

46. Lion Maggots Eat Lion Meat

When I was in Taiwan, after each ceremony, I would usually give blessings to all the believers by mo-ding.

Once, during mo-ding, I suddenly felt that there was a male watching me with a sideways glare. This male was outside of the queue line of worshippers.

This male's appearance, at first glance, was:

1. The hair and facial hair were untidy.
2. He was about half a century old.
3. He wore strange clothing.
4. His eyes were giving off an evil aura.

Upon seeing him, a voice told me, "Something will happen to him sooner or later. Lion maggots eat lion meat!"

I was secretly startled in my heart, but I did not pay attention to it.

It was said that this man called himself a psychic and could give people consultations. Although he had taken refuge under me, he did not truly abide by the rules and disciplines, nor did he cultivate diligently. He was only stopping by.

Later, something really happened.

He broke a national law.

From this incident, I would like to write an article to warn the people of this world.

I have made a vow:

"To not forsake a single being!"

That is, if anyone wishes to take refuge in me, I will never refuse him or her, and will accept all.

That is why my disciples are a mix of good and bad. There are the most outstanding disciples, but there are also disciples with inferior character. Scumbags, the common, and the holy, are all available. So, in reality I have too many disciples.

Among my disciples, I have both lawbreakers and law-abiders. There are those who have been hoodlums or prostitutes. I also have convicts who take refuge in me. There are blackmailers, robbers, drug traffickers, sex offenders, etc…

In female prison, we also have masters [who visit in prison] to spread the dharma. Many convicts, male and female, have taken refuge.

As everyone knows,"Convicts sentenced to death have sariras." It is clear that I even take in death-row convicts for disciples.

My teaching method is just like this!

Precisely because it is like this, it is difficult for me, as a master, to avoid being encumbered by all the various disciples.

Some disciples, who although have taken refuge in me, still have inherent bad habits. These bad habits are not completely gotten rid of. Even people who are trying to gradually get rid of their bad habits, still have natures of greed, anger, and ignorance. They are not able to supersede the ordinary and enter into the sanctified state [of being] in such a short time.

Even though I am patient, they are not listening.

I use the greatest compassionate power of the buddhas and bodhisattvas, as well as wisdom's teaching, and dharma power's teaching, hoping that disciples are able to achieve "yogic union" with various Vajrayana deities, and in this way save sentient beings.

I always emphasize:

True Buddha School is a most rational religion which is well-grounded in humanity, reason, and the law.

All [activities are done] under the tenets of humanity, rationality, and laws, to propagate the Buddha's compassion and wisdom.

Disciples who have taken refuge need to abide by the laws.

Disciples who have taken refuge need to abide by the Vajrayana precepts. Not only abide by the "Five Precepts," "Eight Precepts," "Bodhisattva Vows," "Bhiksu Precepts," "Bhiksuni Precepts," but even the "The Fifty Stanzas of Guru Devotion," "The Fourteen Vajrayana Root Precepts," and so on.

Vajrayana has more precepts compared to Sutrayana.

Our True Buddha School places emphasis on precepts. If precepts are broken, one must properly repent until one sees "the manifestations of repentance." To acknowledge and correct one's actions, thereupon, is the greatest blessing!

We emphasize:

Great Homage Practice.

Great Offering Practice.

Great Refuge Practice.

Great Repentance Practice.

Generation of the greatest bodhicitta.

I hope and expect that disciples who have committed wrongdoings, to accept the law's enforcement of punishment; not only should they receive punishment, they should also repent, and to never repeat the wrongdoing. I want all disciples to abide by the law, to abide by the precepts, and to never ever act recklessly!

Everyone needs to know the laws and to never ever break them. Everyone should know the precepts and be sure to always uphold them. Only in this way can one not go against [the principle of] "a singular mind in kindness" of which we are aware during our refuge-taking.

47. A Letter of Gratitude

Dear Respected Buddha Master,

Disciple Lianhua Yuanyuan and my little daughter, Lianhua Xinyue, pay homage and prostrate to you, the most precious holy master, Living Buddha Lian-sheng!

"*Om, gu-ru, lian-sheng, sid-dhi, hum*!"

Disciple would forever not forget the 15th day of the 8th lunar month of this year, which was also the day of the Mid-Autumn Festival. My daughter Lianhua Xinyue's headache had suddenly intensified and we immediately sent her to the hospital to do a series of tests. After almost three weeks later, no causes could be found.

My child would have severe headaches throughout the day; at night, the pain would worsen to the point that she would bash her own head. As she was unable to sleep, her body became weak and emaciated. Her eyes became dull, without life, and her face took on a pale and green tinge. The tormenting pain grinded her mercilessly and we were powerless to help the pitiful child. I bewailed my inability to protect her as a mother. I would be willing to lay my life down if it meant saving her!

After going through many setbacks, at last, with the help of the buddhas and bodhisattvas, we were lucky to get in touch with dharma sister Chan of Vancouver. With dharma sister Chan's valuable assistance and arrangement, we became primary supplicants of homa offerings. By October 2, we were finally able to personally deliver our letter and photograph to Grand Master, beseeching his blessing.

I only saw Grand Master say softly, "Avalokitesvara Bodhisattva will be in charge." Then he took my child's photograph and pressed it on his forehead. This seemed like a casual gesture, but to my child it had an incomparably significant and profound meaning. An endless stream of powerful and invisible super dharma blessed her. After that, my daughter's headache symptom finally disappeared.

As I watched her carrying her backpack and excitedly head to school, her adorable face once again showed the smile which had been absent for a long time. How can this disciple not be grateful for Grand Master's life-saving kindness? No words can express this feeling of gratitude!

Later, in the evening of the 17th of October, I dreamt and saw that Grand Master personally came to my house to bless it. In the dream, Grand Master was pinching disciple's nose, and squeezing out a small amount of secretion. After that dream, when I blew my nose, a pile of dense phlegm-like substance was expelled. A few days later, I pleasantly discovered that the allergic rhinitis that had been plaguing me for many years had vanished without treatment!

Over and over again, the facts showed that Grand Master is Buddha! It is the truth with no deception! The pure, bright buddha light shines and blesses us, allowing us to escape suffering! Grand Master saved our child, and also saved our whole family!

How extraordinary is Grand Master's blessing power! As a True Buddha disciple, I am fortunate. I am unreservedly proud and blessed to be able to take refuge in Buddha Master!

With Grand Master's rescue, I am even more aware how frightful cause and effect is! Human life is suffering, life is frail and momentary!

If one does not follow Grand Master's teachings and seriously cultivate and seek the fundamental way to liberation, one is squandering human life massively!

Disciple, Lianhua Yuanyuan, again with daughter, Lianhua Xinyue, bow in deep gratitude to Grand Master!

Although I do not know how to express my feelings of gratitude to Grand Master with beautiful rhetoric and language, I am willing to wholeheartedly offer my action [body], speech, and mind to Grand Master. [I am willing] to follow Grand Master in cultivation life after life, dutifully undertake bodhi activities, and promote the Buddhadharma and save sentient beings within my meagre means!

I wish Buddha Master stay in good health, turn the great dharma wheel, succour all sentient beings, and not enter nirvana!

Disciple Lianhua Yuanyuan and family in prostration.
Om, gu-ru, lian-sheng, sid-dhi, hum.
October 25, 2011

And:
A verse of gratitude from someone who recovered from cancer:

Paying homage at Buddha's feet:
Great Doctor King Buddha who is adept at healing sickness.
I now send up to you a most majestic salute.
Having cancer, the body and mind was uneasy.
Buddha Master came to my dream at night.
To say the realization of dependent origination
Is most extraordinary.
And to say objects without dependent origination
Are like empty flowers.
Therefore, a cancer tumor does not exist without conditions.
Saying to stretch out your precious hand

Like searching in a pocket to retrieve something.
Extracting the sickness
Resulting from evil conditions from within my body.
Now everything is gone without a trace.
In this life, only you are unmatched and unrivalled.

Gratitude! Gratitude! Gratitude!
December 17, 2011
Lianhua Yingcheng, a hundred prostrations.

48. Spiritual Response after Blessing by Mo-Ding

The first example:

Lianhua Yintang said:

I held out my "Red Jambhala" for Grand Master Lu to touch the head of "Red Jambhala." I saw him [also] recite one phrase, "*Om, ga-na-ba-di-ye, so-hạ.*"

When I went back home, I smelled an exotic fragrance. The fragrance drifted about the entire shrine and did not disperse even after one week. I had never smelled this type of fragrance before in my life. It was truly too miraculous.

As a result:

"I won a special prize!"

The second example:

Lianhua Yizheng said:

I was six months pregnant and the ultrasound showed that the fetus' position was not normal. The doctor advised that I should do more exercises so as to move the infant to a normal position. The doctor warned that giving birth would be difficult if I did not do so.

I was very worried upon hearing this. So I went up Tiger Mountain, to Taiwan Lei Zang Temple, and listened to Grand Master Lu's discourse on the *Platform Sutra of the Sixth Patriarch.*

During mo-ding, I requested Grand Master Lu to touch my belly. He lightly patted once and said, "It is fine now!"

After two days, I went to my principal doctor for an ultrasonic examination.

The principal doctor said, "The fetus' position is normal!"

Actually, I had not really started doing any exercises, and the fetus' position had become normal. Thank you, Grand Master Lu.

The third example:

Lianhua Shuangshuang said:

I had cataracts and had arranged for a removal surgery to be performed on a certain day and time.

During Grandmaster Lu's mo-ding, I casually asked, "Grand Master Lu, please touch my eyes." I saw Grand Master Lu touch my eyes casually—it was a light brush of the hand, before moving on.

During the pre-surgery examination, the doctor suddenly said, "The cataracts are gone!"

I was baffled when I heard this!

I asked, "How could they disappear?"

The doctor could not provide an explanation.

The fourth example:

Lianhua Nengci said:

Once, Grand Master Lu was giving me mo-ding. He patted the crown of my head two times. Usually he only pats once, but this time round, he did it twice. I reasoned that he patted me the second time because I did not stand up right away after the first one!

That day, when I returned home to cultivate, I noticed it was different than before. A gush of pure energy spread from the crown of my head downwards. The whole body felt as if it was getting an electric shock; it was filled with the bliss of the dharma. I felt at ease, with a feeling of lightness.

This feeling of comfort and ease did not just take place during cultivation. Even after the cultivation session ended, it continued to be present, and there was no doubt about it. The emergence of this secret sensation was continuously present. It was really too wonderful for words!

Thank you Grand Master Lu!

The fifth example:

Lianhua Yijia said:

During the mo-ding, I held out my mala beads for Grand Master Lu to touch. After returning home, I placed the mala beads on the shrine. When I turned off the lights, the shrine emitted rainbow brilliance.

When I looked again, I realize that the light was actually coming from the mala beads. The rays of light had many colors. This was something I had never seen before. Was there something wrong with my eyes? I looked [at the scenery] outside the window and everything was normal. Then I looked at the shrine again, and rainbow colors were still there. This rainbow brilliance remained for seven days before fading off.

The sixth example:

Lianhua Dejin said:

When Grand Master was giving mo-ding, I visualized that my father also receive the mo-ding. As he had just passed away, my heart was stricken with grief. I wondered where he was reincarnated to?

Unexpectedly, that night, I saw my father in my dream.

My father said to me:

Your master has already delivered me to the pure land and you do not need to worry anymore. At the very moment you were receiving mo-ding, I entered the Buddha land.

My father was happy and young.
My father said from his own mouth, “Your master is a Buddha.”

49. The Secret to Generating Faith

In writing this book, *Open Your Mind*, I hope to "generate faith" in everyone. This is the purpose of writing this book.

For me, "writing" and "cultivation" are the core themes of my life. It has always been this way without change, from my youth to the age of sixty-seven.

My life is all about Buddhadharma.

About others:

"I do not have anything else!"

Buddhadharma starts from faith. That is why having authored two hundred and twenty-six books, I still write about "generating faith," because "faith is the mother of all achievements and virtue."

Over these past years, because my mind has been frank and unattached—not wanting anything and not being bothered by anything, I have entered a state of purity and ease. I feel very contented with my life, and feel that life should be just like this. The worries of the past have been wiped clean. Now, when I look upon this world, it is with an even incisive insight. After realizing my mind and seeing my Buddha-nature:

"I enter quietude instantaneously."

I understand Buddhadharma's:

Emptiness.

Nature of Emptiness.

Distinction in the Nature of Emptiness.

I understand:

Prajna.

Contemplation of the Middle Way.

Consciousness-only.

This book, is a "faith-generating" book. Hence, it is a book on an expedient method leading to the gate of cultivation. The way I see it, even though there are so many incidents of spiritual responses, I use the true stories of these spiritual responses to guide people to enter the state of the "correct faith" of the Buddhadharma.

The Five Aggregates are empty in nature.

Entering profound samadhi, one understands that all dharma is like emptiness.

I!

Although I know that all Buddha lands are "illusory," I am able to, through pure marvelous actions, dignify Buddha lands.

Although I know that buddhas and bodhisattvas are also "illusory," I am able to, through pure marvelous actions, dignify buddhas and bodhisattvas.

Although I know that human life is "illusory," I am able to, through pure marvelous actions, beautify one's life.

Although I know that cause and effect, reincarnation, and nirvana, are all "illusory," I am able to, through purified marvelous actions, explain about them.

I already know:

All dharmas are uniformly void and tranquil, neither arising nor cessation. Birth, death and nirvana, ordinary beings and all buddhas, are but appearances of flowers in the sky.

(This is the pinnacle of emptiness.)

But:

I use illusory means to commence a person's firm belief. Otherwise, words cannot describe the emptiness and tranquility of Buddha-nature. In accordance to the differences among sentient beings, I expound different dharmas.

Nagarjuna's *Fundamental Verses on the Middle Way (The Mulamadhyamakakarika)*:

All things (dharmas) arising from causes and conditions, I say are simply emptiness, which are also false names, which is also the meaning of the Middle Way.

Those for whom emptiness is possible, for them everything is possible. Those for whom emptiness is not possible, for them everything is not possible.

There has never been a thing (dharma), that does not arise from causes and conditions. Therefore, all things (dharmas), are empty.

Shakyamuni Buddha is also known as "King of Emptiness Buddha."

The *Platform Sutra of the Sixth Patriarch* has a few important phrases, that are also like this:

The wonderful nature of worldly people is originally empty, and there is not a single dharma which can be obtained. The true emptiness of the self-nature is also like this.

To realize that the three bodies have no self-nature, is to understand the four wisdoms of Bodhi.

Your original nature, like the void, has nothing visible, is the correct view; while nothing that can be known, is true suchness.

Since realizing my mind and seeing my Buddha-nature, I only know two words:

1. Emptiness.
2. Illusion.

However, this kind of realization, is obtained from in-depth study and relentless practice of the Buddhadharma for forty years in the human realm. If human birth is not obtained as a result of causes and conditions; if an in-depth investigation of the Buddhadharma is not performed as a result of causes and conditions; if faith is not commenced as a result of causes and conditions; if yogic responses are not obtained as a result of causes and conditions; if supernatural abilities are not possible due to causes and conditions; if wisdom does not arise due to causes and conditions; How do I become liberated?

Buddha is beyond this mundane world, believe it!

GLOSSARY

-A-

Action Tantra (Kriyatantra)
In Sanskrit, "Kriyatantra." The first of four levels of tantra emphasizing external action or ritual over the practice of meditation. The other levels in ascending order are Conduct or Performance Tantra (Caryatantra), Yoga Tantra (Yogatantra), and Highest Yoga Tantra (Anuttarayogatantra).

Affinity
A relationship by fate or destiny, is a Buddhist-related Chinese concept that means the predetermined principle that dictates a person's relationships and encounters, such as the affinity among family, friends, or lovers. In common usage the term can be defined as the "binding force" that links two people together in any relationship. It is also used to explain events occurring in people's lives. The driving forces and causes behind affinity are created as a result of previous lives.

Alaya Consciousness (Sanskrit, literally "Abode, Dwelling")
The alaya-consciousness is usually described as the "seed bed," where all the "seeds" of good and bad karmas are stored, so it is also called "store-house consciousness." This eighth consciousness stores all the actions and experiences from one's lives as karmas. It is unaffected by the death of one's physical body. Hence, karmas follow one from lives to lives exerting influence on the working of seven consciousnesses.

Amitabha Buddha (Sanskrit, literally "Boundless light")
The Buddha of Boundless Light and Longevity, he is one of the Five Wisdom Buddhas and the Lord of the Lotus Family. He embodies

the Wisdom of Discerning Awareness which is the antidote to desire and lust. Amitabha Buddha's pure land (paradise) is called Sukhavati and is located in the western direction. He is the Primary Buddha of the Pure Land Sect and often depicted to be accompanied by his two attendants, Avalokitesvara Bodhisattva and Mahasthamaprapta Bodhisattva.

Amitabha Sutra
A popular colloquial name for the *Shorter Sukhavativyuha Sutra.* The *Amitabha Sutra* is a Mahayana sutra and is one of the three primary texts of Pure Land Buddhism, along with the *Infinite Life Sutra* and the *Amitayurdhyana Sutra.*

Animal Release Ritual
"Animal Release" is a term used by Chinese Buddhists to refer to the practice of purchasing animals that are due to be slaughtered and letting them to go back into the wild. The rationale of this practice is the Buddha's teaching of kindness, compassion, and benevolence to all creatures.

Avalokitesvara Bodhisattva
(Sanskrit, literally "Lord Who Observes Sounds of the World")
The embodiment of compassion, Avalokitesvara Bodhisattva compassionately observes the sounds of the world and renders assistance to any devotee who calls out his name. The stories of prayers answered and the myriad miracles performed by Avalokitesvara made him the most widely worshipped bodhisattva. Known as Chenrezig in Tibet, the Tibetan people claim to be his descendents and consider him as their patron bodhisattva. They believe that Chenrezig has appeared many times in Tibet to protect the Buddhist faith. King Songtsan Gampo (the Tibetan king who introduced Buddhism into Tibet) and Dalai Lama are believed by Tibetans to be incarnations

of Chenrezig. As result of this special relationship, Avalokitesvara's mantra, "Om Mani Padme Hum," is the most widely chanted mantra by the Tibetan people.

Avici Hell
The eighth and most painful of the eight Buddhist hells. It is the lowest level of the hells, in which suffering is the greatest and longest.

-B-

Bardo Deliverance
This practice is to assist spirits who are between rebirths (in the bardo state). With this practice, spirits are able to attain a higher level of rebirth. A bardo deliverance ceremony may be done for ancestors and other spirits.

Bhiksu
A male practitioner who has renounced worldly life and taken the pledge to observe approximately 250 precepts of a fully ordained monk in order to attain liberation from samsara.

Bhiksuni
A female practitioner who has renounced worldly life and taken the pledge to observe the 500 precepts of a fully ordained nun in order to attain liberation from samsara.
Bodhi
A Sanskrit term used for enlightenment. The term is generally applied to those individuals who have understood the effectiveness of four noble truths and achieved the results of completing the eightfold path. The spiritual condition of a buddha or bodhisattva.

Bodhicitta (Sanskrit, literally "Awakened Mind"; Bodhi Mind)

The key to Mahayana Buddhism, it refers both to an enlightened mind and to the resolution arising from the profound compassion to attain an enlightened mind for the purpose of assisting all beings.

Bodhisattva
(Sanskrit, literally "Enlightenment-being with Compassion")
One who has developed the altruistic motive of dedicating his existence throughout all rebirths to the attainment of enlightenment in order to liberate other beings who are suffering in samsara (the cycle of karma and reincarnation).

Bodhisattva Vows
A set of twenty-eight vows taken by those who aspire Bodhisattvahood or Buddhahood.

Brahma (The Creator)
One of the three primary deities of Hinduism. The other two deities are Vishnu (the preserver) and Shiva (the destroyer). He is usually depicted with four heads, four faces, and four arms. Buddhist scriptures recorded that Brahma (called "Indra" in the sutras) appeared to Shakyamuni Buddha after the Buddha's enlightenment. Brahma asked the Buddha not to enter nirvana immediately and stay in the human world to spread Buddha-dharma. Hence, Brahma was the first who requested the Buddha to "turn the dharma wheel."

Buddha (Sanskrit, literally "Awakened One")
The term is typically used to refer to the historical Buddha, Shakyamuni Buddha. In Mahayana Buddhism, the term is not restricted to just Shakyamuni Buddha, but may refer to anyone who is enlightened.

Buddhadharma
Buddha doctrine or the teachings of the Buddha.

Buddha-nature
The inherent nature of all sentient beings. All sentient beings have the potential to awaken their buddha-nature and become buddhas.

Buddha Pure Land
A spiritual realm of consciousness. Each buddha has their own pure land and one may vow to go to that pure land upon death. When one is reborn in a pure land, one may proceed on the path of spiritual development until enlightenment is achieved.

-C-

Cause and Effect
A foundational concept in Buddhist, Hindu, Jain and Sikh traditions, it is believed that all actions, thoughts, and speech generate a result. If one is virtuous in body, speech, and mind, then one will have good fortune, harmonious relationships, success, happiness, etc. If one performs non-virtuous deeds of body, speech, or mind, one will suffer the consequences. The results of one's deeds, good or bad, will bear fruit in the present life or in future lives. The experiences one currently witnesses are a result of previous actions of past lives, or even from actions committed previously in this current life. Karma, or cause and effect, is what drives the cycle of reincarnation for all sentient beings.

Channels (Mai)
Channels are subtle energy paths through which qi (wind) and drops flow. The three main channels are the central channel (sushumna), the left (ida) and the right (pingala) channels which run parallel to and in front of the spinal column.

City God (Cheng Huang)
A common Taoist deity who controls the spirits within a certain area (a town or city).

Conduct Tantra (Caryatantra)
In Sanskrit, "Caryatantra," also known as Performance Tantra. The second of four levels of tantra emphasizing both external rituals and internal yoga. It is ranked above Action Tantra (Kriyatantra), but below Yoga Tantra (Yogatantra) and Highest Yoga Tantra (Anuttarayogatantra).

Consciousness
Also translated as mind and discernment, consciousness is the translation of Sanskrit *vijnana*. Consciousness in this usage does not refer to the mind. Instead, it refers to the sensory based perception and the mind. In early schools of Buddhism, they speak of only six consciousnesses: eye (sight) consciousness, ear (hearing) consciousness, nose (smell) consciousness, tongue (taste) consciousness, body (tactile) consciousness, and mind consciousness. These six consciousnesses together shape our understanding of reality. In the Yogacara School, the six consciousnesses were expanded to eight consciousnesses, and later, nine and ten consciousnesses.

Consciousness Transference Yoga
(Bardo Transference of Consciousness Yoga or Phowa Practice)
A Vajrayana Buddhist meditation practice and also one of the Six Yogas of Naropa. The method can be applied at the moment of death to, according to Vajrayana Buddhist belief, transfer one's consciousness through the top of the head directly into a Buddha-field of one's choice. By doing so, one bypasses some of the typical experiences that are said to occur after death.

Consecration (Eye Opening Ceremony)
After a Buddhist altar is set up, a practitioner may have a vajra master or reverend perform this ceremony so that the respective deities on the altar descend and thus become "alive."

Cultivation
The practices one does in order to purify karma, to purify oneself of greed, anger, and ignorance, to create merit, to generate bodhicitta and, ultimately, to achieve enlightenment.

-D-

Dakini (Sanskrit, literally "Space-goer")
An accomplished female divine being who has attained the clear light and assists Vajrayana practitioners in removing physical hindrances and spiritual obstacles. As they are female beings that travel in space, they are linked with giving birth to the full range of expansive potentialities.

Dependent Origination
Dependent Origination states that all dharmas ("things") arise in dependence upon other dharmas: "if this exists, that exists; if this ceases to exist, that also ceases to exist." The principle is applied in the twelve links of dependent origination doctrine in Buddhism, which describes the chain of causes which result in rebirth and dukkha (suffering). See *Twelve Links of Dependent Origination.*

Dharani
Originally, it could be a seed syllable, a mantra, a sutra, or sastra. A practitioner would recite it to help increase memory, increase wisdom, decipher right from wrong, allow one to not be angered, and would teach one the forty-two root seed syllable sounds. In modern times, it

is generally referring to a long mantra.

Dharma

Typically, "dharma" is used to describe the body of teachings expounded by the Buddha. However, the word is also used in Buddhist phenomenology as the term for phenomenon, a basic unit of existence and/or experience.

Dharma Protector (Vajra Protector; Wrathful Protector; Dharmapala)

An enlightened being that takes on a wrathful form and whose function is to protect Buddhist practitioners.

Dharma Wheel

An eight spoke wheel used as a symbol to represent the teachings of Buddhism. "Turning the dharma wheel" means to teach and spread Buddhist teachings.

Divine Eye (Heavenly Eye)

The divine eye is a faculty of devas in the Realm of Form that perceives both far and near, inside and outside, as well as day and night. It is a faculty which can be acquired through two ways (as mentioned by Shakyamuni Buddha, recorded in the *Mahaprajnaparamitasastra* by Nagarjuna) through the ripening of seeds sown in previous lives, or as a result of spiritual cultivation in one's current life.

Divination

The process of obtaining answers to questions through divine sources such as buddhas, bodhisattvas, and gods.

Diting the Unicorn Beast

The sacred beast upon which Ksitigarbha Bodhisattva sits. It is a unicorn that resembles a lion.

Drops (Light Drops)
This is a transcription of "Bindu." In tantric philosophy, physical bodily fluids are seen as being the most material manifestations of substances that also express themselves in rarefied or subtle forms. Collectively, the full range of these substances is known as "Bodhicitta," a term which also signifies will to enlightenment or compassion. Individual drops of this are termed "Bindu."

-E-

Earth Deity
A Taoist deity who protects the area around a house or temple. He is said to be the Earth God of Wealth and Merit.

Eight Precepts
Including the five precepts, these are: (1) no killing; (2) no stealing; (3) no sex; (4) no lying; (5) no drinking alcohol or taking intoxicants; (6) no wearing perfumes, cosmetics or adornments, no singing, dancing, no listening or playing music or watching song and dance entertainment; (7) no sitting on high and luxurious places or sleeping on a luxurious bed; and (8) no eating after lunch, until morning.

Emperor Liang Repentance
A major Buddhist repentance service named after the Emperor Liang. The repentance records and details the reasons behind his wife's transformation, examples of people affected by karma, stories about people receiving retribution, and what one can do to prevent it. The repentance also involves prostrations to a number of Buddhas.

Empowerment
A ritual wherein the guru transmits to a student the energy of a particular deity or practice so that the student's practice may quickly

bear fruit.

Esoteric
Pertaining to Vajrayana, Tantric, Tantrayana, Mantrayana, Secret Mantra, Diamond Way, Thunderbolt Way, or Indestructible Way.

Expedient Means (Skillful Means)
Methods and teachings to help people understand and bring them closer to authentic dharma, and ultimately bring them to enlightenment. For example, the Jambhala practices entice one to practice to increase one's wealth, and the result is that one learns Buddhism, the dharma, one's wisdom increases, and, eventually, this individual is brought closer to enlightenment through this expedient practice.

-F-

Feng Shui (Geomancy; Chinese, literally "Wind Water")
Use of astronomy and geography in placement of buildings, gardens, water features, furniture, objects, etc. to help one improve life by receiving positive energy. It is an art and science which originated in China approximately three thousand years ago.

Fifty Stanzas of Guru Devotion (Gurupancasika)
Written by Master Asvaghosa, this work defines the etiquette disciples must adopt to show their respect to their guru. Disciples of Vajrayana Buddhism must follow these rules and show utmost dedication to their guru if they hope to have accomplishment in their practices.

Five Aggregates (Five Skandhas)
"Skandha" is Sanskrit for "aggregates." The five skandhas are: form, feeling, perception, mental formation, and consciousness. These

are psychophysical components of a human being which, when interacting together, create the illusion of self and inherent existence of self.

Five Precepts
The most basic precepts of Buddhism: (1) do not kill; (2) do not steal; (3) do not commit sexual misconduct; (4) do not lie; (5) and do not take intoxicants.

Four Enlightened Realms (Four Holy Realms)
The realms of sravaka, pratyekabuddha, bodhisattva, and buddha.

-G-

Garbhadhatu (Womb Mandala)
One of the two major mandalas in the Shingon School (Japanese Tantric Buddhism). It represents the material world, the static part of the cosmos. It contains all, protects all and nourishes everything.

Garuda
Great golden-winged birds. They are considered to be half animal and half god. They used to eat dragons from the ocean until the Dragon King pleaded to the Buddha to have him help convince the garudas to stop eating the dragons. The Buddha agreed to have all reverends make daily offerings to the garudas in exchange for not eating anymore dragons. They serve as protectors and helpers to dharma practitioners.

Gelug/Gelugpa/Yellow Sect
Known as the Yellow Sect because of the large yellow hats worn by the reverends during ceremonies, this is the most popular school currently in Tibet and surrounding regions. The founder of Gelug, Tsongkhapa (1367-1419 AD) received teachings from Nyingma,

Kagyu, Sakya and other schools. Tsongkhapa was well known for his strict observance of the monastic disciplines as set forth in the Vinaya. In the mid sixteenth century, Sonam Gyatso, the second reincarnation of Tsongkhapa's main disciple was later bestowed the title "Dalai" (Mongolian for "ocean") and the institution of Dalai Lama was created.

Golden Mother of the Jade Pond

Ruler of all female immortals, she is the most important female deity of the Taoist Pantheon. Known by many names such as Queen Mother of the West, she came into being from the gathering of primordial yin (feminine) energy. Her palace is located on top a peak in the Kunlun Mountain Range. She represents the metal element in the Taoists Five Elements (metal, wood, water, fire, and earth) and there is a Jade Pond near her palace, hence she is also known as the Jade Pond Golden Mother.

Great Compassion Repentance

The Great Compassion Repentance is based on the Great Compassion Mantra (Da Bei Zhou). The full name of the Great Compassion Mantra literally means, "Thousand-arms and thousand-eyes Avalokitesvara Bodhisattva's all embracing great compassion Dharani." The mantra consists of eighty-four phrases. It is very popular in the Chinese culture, and widely recited among devotees.

Green Tara

Tara is a female Bodhisattva in Mahayana Buddhism who appears as a female Buddha in Vajrayana Buddhism. Within Tibetan Buddhism, Tara is regarded as a Bodhisattva of compassion and action. She is the female aspect of Avalokitesvara and in some stories she comes from his tears. There are many forms of Tara, and the Green Tara and White Tara are the most popular representations of Tara.

Great Exposition of Secret Mantra

Written by Tsongkhapa, it is one of the principal classic texts on tantra. It presents the main features common to all the Buddhist tantra systems as well as the differences between sutra and tantra. In it, Tsongkhapa covers paths to Buddhahood, vajra vehicle, deity yoga, and method in the four tantras and details the practices of Action and Performance Tantra.

Guru

Two Sanskrit words - "gu" means darkness and "ru" means light. Therefore, a guru is one who can lead the student from darkness to light - from ignorance to wisdom. In Vajrayana Buddhism, the guru (teacher) is the first and foremost element of one's level of accomplishment. This teacher gives the practitioner the lineage blessing of all past lineage gurus. The guru has also learned, practiced and attained accomplishments in his or her teachings. With the guidance of an authentic guru, one may more quickly reach enlightenment.

Guru Mantra

The Heart Mantra of Padmakumara (Living Buddha Lian-sheng): *Om, gu-ru, lian-sheng, sid-dhi, hum.*

-H-

Hariti

As told in *The Lotus Sutra*, she was a cannibalistic demon who had hundreds of children, but abducted, killed, and ate the children of others. The bereaved mothers of her victims went to Shakyamuni Buddha to ask him to put a stop to her murders. The Buddha stole Hariti's youngest child and hid him under a begging bowl. She went to the Buddha for help and he made her understand how it felt to have one's child missing and asked if she could imagine the suffering of parents whose children had been devoured. Shakyamuni told her that from then on all reverends would make offerings to her on a daily basis to satisfy her hunger and thirst so that she would not eat the children of others.

High King Avalokitesvara Sutra (*High King Sutra*)
This sutra includes the names of many buddhas and bodhisattvas of the three times and ten directions and has been in circulation since the Tang Dynasty. To chant the *High King Avalokitesvara Sutra* is equivalent to receiving blessings and empowerment from the buddhas and bodhisattvas of the three times and ten directions.

Highest Yoga Tantra (Annutarayogatantra)
This is the highest teaching of the Gelugpa sect of Tibetan Buddhism. The practitioner utilizes subtle levels of bodily energies and consciousness, which are not accessible to the untrained practitioner, to achieve complete Buddhahood.

Homa (Fire Offering, Fire Puja)
A fire ritual used as a means of offering to buddhas, bodhisattvas, dharma protectors or spiritual beings. They are performed in order to increase merit, eradicate negative karma, increase wealth, harmony and good health.

-I-

-J-

Jade Emperor
The Jade Emperor in Chinese culture, traditional religions and myth is one of the representations of the first god. In Taoist theology he is Yuanshi Tianzun, one of the Three Pure Ones, the three primordial

emanations of the Tao.

Jambhala (God of Wealth)
There are five Jambhalas: (1) the White Jambhala; (2) the Red Jambhala; (3) the Yellow Jambhala; (4) the Green Jambhala; (5) the Black Jambhala. The Yellow Jambhala is a principal deity in the True Buddha School and is seen as an eighth level Bodhisattva. Jambhalas are able to grant abundance to those practicing his dharma, allowing the individual to practice the Buddhadharma and to help others.

-K-

Kagyu/Kagyupa/White Sect
This school became known as the White Sect due to Milarepa, one of the lineage gurus, dressing in a simple white cotton robe when he was in retreat. The sect was founded by lineage gurus beginning with Tilopa to Naropa to Marpa and then to his disciple Milarepa. Nevertheless, it flourished especially during the time of Milarepa's most famous disciple, Gampopa. After Gampopa, it soon fractioned into many sub-sects, known as the Four Great and Eight Minors, headed by Gampopa's chief disciples. It is especially known for its meditation and yogic practices.

Kalachakra (Sanskrit, literally "Wheel of Time")
This is one of the four Highest Tantra Yoga practices. It is considered to be one of the most complex practices.

Karmapa (Sanskrit, literally "Buddha-Activity Man")
The spiritual head of the Karma Kagyu Sect of Tibetan Buddhism. The first incarnation of the Karmapa was in 1110 AD, making this the longest-lived line of Tibetan Tulkus. Presently, he is in his seventeenth incarnation.

Ksitigarbha Bodhisattva (Sanskrit, literally "Womb of the Earth")
One of the eight mahasattvas (great beings), the bodhisattva of great vows, and like all bodhisattvas, he aspires to deliver sentient beings wandering astray in the six realms (hell denizens, hungry ghosts, animals, asuras, humans, and devas), but he specializes in delivering beings from hell. He is usually represented as a standing venerated figure, holding in his right hand a pilgrim's staff, and in his left a pearl. His famous vow is "Not until the hells are emptied will I become a Buddha; not until all beings are saved will I certify to Bodhi."

-L-

Lake Sammamish
A freshwater lake eight miles east of Seattle in King County, Washington, United States. It is within walking distance from the True Buddha School's Ling Shen Ching Tze Temple in Redmond. In his 60th book, The Inner World of the Lake, Grand Master Lu describes Lake Sammamish under various conditions, in different times and seasons.

Laozi (Lao-Tzu or Lao-Tze) (Chinese, literally "Old Master")
Laozi was an ancient Chinese philosopher and writer. He is known as the reputed author of the *Tao Te Ching* and the founder of philosophical Taoism, and as a deity in religious Taoism and traditional Chinese religions.

Light Drops (Mingdian)
Prana (chi/qi), channels (mai), and light drops (mingdian) are the three key elements in Tantric Buddhist energy practices. See Drops.

Lineage Guru
A lineage typically begins with a human being who is able to communicate with the buddhas, learn their teachings and pass the teachings onto a primary disciple. For example: Vajradhara Buddha taught Tilopa, and then these teachings were then passed to Naropa, Marpa, Milarepa and Gampopa successively. Honoring lineage gurus is a vital element of Vajrayana Buddhism and sadhanas typically begin with visualizing the blessing of the lineage gurus blessing the practitioner.

Lord Yama (Yama King, Yama, Deva, Hell King)
Yama was considered to have been the first mortal who died and espied the way to the celestial abodes, and in virtue of precedence he became the ruler of the departed. Therefore, he is known as the greatest king (Lord) of the netherworld and the head of karmic arbiter giving punishment of those who reside in hell. He is also featured in Brahmanic mythology as the ruler of one of the heavens (or devalokas), the Suyāma Heaven.

Lotus Sutra Repentance
This repentance ritual was created by Master Tian Tai, based on the *Dharma Flower Sutra* [also known as the *Lotus Sutra*]. It is also referred to as the *Repentance of the Six Roots* or the *Dharma Flower Samaya Repentance.*

-M-

Maha Twin Lotus Ponds
This is the pure land of Padmakumara located in the Western Paradise of Amitabha. By practicing the True Buddha Tantra, one may travel to the Maha Twin Lotus Ponds in meditation or at the time of death.

Mahamayuri Vidyarajni (the Peacock Dharma Protector)
An emanation of Vairocana Buddha who has the power to create harmony, increase wealth, purify negative karma and protect practitioners from disasters.

Mahapratisara Bodhisattva
A transformation of Guanyin Bodhisattva. Mahapratisara is a deity in the court of Guanyin in the Garbhadhatu mandala of Vajrayana and has the Vajrayana name "Wish Granting Vajra." Mahapratisara Bodhisattva always fulfills the wishes of sentient beings. Mahapratisara is therefore referred to as the "Great Wish Fulfilling Bodhisattva." By hearing, chanting, reading, writing, or propagating the *Mahapratisara Dharani*, one earns the merits of passing through fire without getting burned, never being able to be poisoned, subjugation of one's enemies, breaking out of confinement in prison, and never being in harm's way of dragons and fishes. Subsequently, one will have peace and happiness and not be subjected to hardships and difficulties by the king, etc.

Mahayana Buddhism (Sanskrit, literally "Greater Vehicle")
This style of Buddhism emphasizes the paths and practices of bodhisattvas to altruistically assist sentient beings to attain enlightenment. It consists of sutra and tantra systems for achieving enlightenment. While the sutra system teaches how to go from fundamental ignorance to enlightenment over countless lifetimes, the tantra system teaches one can attain buddhahood in a single lifetime. Pure Land, Zen, Yogacara, Madhyamaka, and Vajrayana are some of the schools of the Mahayana tradition.

Mahesvara (Sanskrit, literally "Great Lord of the Universe")
This is another name for Shiva, one of the three main deities of Hinduism. Known also as the Lord of the Yogis, he is typically

pictured as blue in color with snakes decorating his body sitting in deep meditation with his trident in the background.

Maitreya
He presently resides in the Tushita heaven. He will be the future buddha of this aeon.

Mala (Tibetan prayer beads)
An equivalent term to a Catholic's rosary beads. They are typically used as an aid to keep count on the number of times a mantra/sutra is chanted. Mala can be made of wood, crystals, pearls and other materials. They typically come in 21 or 108 bead-length.

Mandala (Sanskrit, literally "Circle")
It is a symbol which represents the realms of buddhas, bodhisattvas, or dharma protectors. It also represents various energies of particular enlightened states of mind. It may be in two dimensions, as in a painting, or in three dimensions, such as in the placement of sacred objects. The body or even the world at large may be interpreted as a mandala, as they symbolize various aspects of universal energies. The representations are very artistic with intricate colors and designs to aid in visualization. It also refers to a visualization of an offering multiplying infinitely into the space of the entire universe.

Manjushri Bodhisattva Rebirth Mantra
This is the rebirth mantra of Manjushri: *Om, ah-bei-la-hum, kan-cha-la, so-ha*. This Rebirth Mantra should be recited by both vegetarians and non-vegetarians. True Buddha School practitioners recite this mantra before eating. Recitation is accompanied by visualization and mudra. By doing so, all of the bardo spirits of the sentient beings (cows, pigs, insects, etc.) within the food are either delivered to the

Western Paradise (if the practitioner is powerful enough), or at least the bardo spirit of the animal has an increased merit.

Mantra
Chants used for blessing, invocation of buddhas, offering, harmonization, purification, protection, longevity, etc. It is a sound of sacred syllable, word, or group of words and is the embodying of spiritual power. The chanting of mantra is used as a method of meditation to create spiritual transformation. A mantra also represents the pure speech of enlightened beings, buddhas and bodhisattvas. It is one of the three secrets of tathagata (pure body, speech, and mind). In Vajrayana Buddhism, the chanting of the mantra (pure speech) is accompanied by visualization (pure mind) and mudra (pure body) as prescribed in sadhana to transform
ordinary body, speech, and mind of a person to the pure body, speech, and mind of a buddha.

Marpa (1012-97 AD)
Known as the "Great Translator," he travelled from Tibet to India three times to bring back various Tantric Buddhist teachings, especially those of his guru, Naropa.

Mazu
The Chinese goddess of the sea believed to have the ability to protect those who face danger on the water. She is an important deity of coastal regions and islands of Southeast Asia. There are at least 509 temples in Taiwan recorded as dedicated wholly or in part to Mazu. In Taiwan, many festivals and ceremonies are held around the third lunar month to honor her birthday.

Medicine Vaidurya Light King Buddha
The founder of the Eastern Paradise of Lapis Lazuli (Vaidurya) Light.

This buddha is the Great Medicine Buddha King who can cure all kinds of sickness. His pure land is the "Pure Land of Lapis Lazuli (Vaidurya) Light," which is highly refined, exquisite and dignified. The mightiness of Medicine Buddha lies in his twelve great vows. One of these vows is to treat the eighty four thousand illnesses of sentient beings by using eighty four thousand medicines so that sentient beings who are sick will have the karma causing the sickness totally eradicated.

Merits
Good karmic fortune created by virtuous deeds and actions. Throughout one's lifetime one accumulates merits based on the deeds one performs. One may also dedicate and transfer merit to another person, the deceased, an ancestor, or any sentient being.
Middle Way (Madhyamaka)
Nagarjuna founded the Middle Way School based on the teachings of emptiness that all things are empty of inherent existence.

Mo-ding
An act of blessing when the guru or acharya places his hand upon the head of the person receiving a blessing.

Moonlight Bodhisattva
Medicine Buddha's attendants are "Sunlight Bodhisattva" and "Moonlight Bodhisattva." When invoking Medicine Buddha these two attendants must also be named at the same time.

Mulamadhyamakakarika
Nagarjuna's Fundamental Verses on the Middle Way. The verses propose the Middle Way which is not partial to existence or non-existence, creation or non-creation, emptiness or non-emptiness.

Mudra (Sanskrit, literally "Seal")
It is an expression of hands and fingers that corresponds to the enlightened body of the three secrets of tathagata (enlightened body, speech, and mind). In meditational practices, forming mudra assists the practitioner to correspond his body with enlightened body of the personal deity. In application, mudra acts as a seal reinforcing the power of mantra and visualization.

-N-

Nagarjuna (second century AD)
He was born into a Brahmin family in southern India. He could commit any sutra to memory. After renunciation he completed reading the three Buddhist canons in ninety days and gained penetration into all profound doctrines. Since his ancestral link could be traced to the nagas or dragons of northern India, he was able to enter the dragon palace under the ocean and study all the Mahayana scriptures that were being kept there, make records, and bring the scriptures back. This was the reason why Mahayana Buddhism flourished. He was taught by Vajrasattva and from these teachings he wrote *The Madhyamika Sastra*, which later became the most important sastra for the Three Sastra School. Since he received the lineage from Vajrasattva, the official establishment of Tantrayana named him as its founder.

Nagas (Sanskrit, literally "Serpent")
These serpent-like spiritual beings living in caves, rivers, and heavens, are known as protectors, benefactors, and a source of wealth. During the Buddha's cultivation of enlightenment, a naga appeared and served the Buddha as a protector from the elements. In Chinese, naga is equated with the Chinese dragon "long."

Nairatmya
Nairatmya (Wu-wo Fomu in Chinese) is also called Vajra Nairatmya Buddha Mother, Vajra Nairatmya Mother, Nairatmya Mother, Nairatmya Consort, or the Mother of all Buddhas. She is the embodiment of prajna wisdom as well as the consort of Hevajra. In Vajrayana, Nairatmya is the Buddha Mother of the Sakya sect.

Namo
Often placed in front of the name of an object of veneration, e.g., a buddha's name or a sutra, to express devotion to it.

Nirvana (Sanskrit, literally "Cessation")
Cessation of suffering where one is freed from the cycle of rebirth. It is a state where one realizes one's connection with the absolute.

Nyingma/Nyingmapa/Red Sect
(Tibetan, literally "School of the Ancients")
This school was founded by Padmasambhava; it is the oldest of the four Tibetan Buddhist schools. It maintains a sophisticated system of study and practice, and its special teaching is Dzogchen.

-O-

Om, gu-ru, lian-sheng, sid-dhi, hum
The Heart Mantra of Padmakumara (Living Buddha Lian-sheng).

-P-

Padma Family of Buddhas (Padmakula)
Refers to one of the Five Buddha Families; headed by Amitabha Buddha.

Padmakumara (Sanskrit, literally "Lotus Youth")
The sambhogakaya (bliss body) form of Living Buddha Lian-sheng, a great fortune-bestowing and hindrance removing Bodhisattva. For more details about Padmakumara and his abode, the Maha Twin Lotus Ponds in the Western Paradise, see The True Buddha Sutra.

Padmasambhava (Sanskrit, literally "Lotus Born")
He is the founder of the Nyingma tradition of Tibetan Buddhism and is commonly known as the Second Buddha, after Shakyamuni Buddha. He was supremely accomplished in the esoteric arts and used his powers to defeat many demons and black magic (Bon) practitioners after being invited by the Tibetan king Trisong Detsen to establish Buddhism in Tibet in the eighth century. Padmasambhava is one of the principal deities of True Buddha School.

Personal Deity (Yidam)
This is a transcription of Yidam, one of the Three Roots (Guru, Yidam and Dharma Protector) of Vajrayana practitioners. One begins to practice the Yidam Yoga after attaining spiritual responses in the Fourfold Preliminary Practices and the Guru Yoga. In meditation, one merges one's consciousness with a Personal Deity. The Personal Deity represents an enlightened state of consciousness and is chosen to correspond to the basic personality of the practitioner. A True Buddha School practitioner chooses one of the eight major deities (Padmakumara, Amitabha Buddha, Avalokitesvara Bodhisattva, Ksitigarbha Bodhisattva, Maha Cundi Bodhisattva, Yellow Jambhala, Padmasambhava, or Medicine Buddha) as the Yidam and practices the personal deity yoga throughout one's lifetime.

Phowa Practice (Tibetan, Literally "Transference of Consciousness")
A tantric practice of transferring one's consciousness through the top of the head directly into a Buddha-realm.

Platform Sutra of the Sixth Patriarch
A Buddhist scripture that was composed in China during the 8th to 13th century. The key topics of the discourse are the direct perception of one's true nature, and the unity in essence of sila, dhyana and prajna.

Prajna
The ultimate wisdom.

Pramanavarttika
Dharmakirti's (an Indian Buddhist scholar) main treatise on pramana. Pramana is a Sanskrit term which is commonly translated as "valid cognition" which means the correct knowledge of a particular object. The Pramanavarttika is considered the most important of his Seven Treatises on Valid Cognition.
Pratyekabuddha (Solitary Realizer)
A practitioner who attains nirvana without a human teacher, but does not go on to teach others the path towards enlightenment.

Precepts
These are rules and vows that Buddhist laity and reverends need to follow in order to eradicate the filth of ignorance in its entirety. A lay devotee has to follow the Five Precepts, the Fourteen Precepts, and others. Monks and nuns adhere to a much more extensive set of precepts. Abiding by these rules inhibits misconduct and fosters virtuous conducts of the body, speech, and mind. They are used to prevent and curb incorrect actions and bad deeds. Stability is attained when the six senses make contact with the external environment but the mind stays still and does not flow along. Wisdom is realized when the mind and the external environment is emptied out and one's views are free from delusions.

Pure Land
A pure abode founded by a buddha. By being reborn in a pure land, the aspirant can continue spiritual development towards enlightenment without fear of falling back into the six realms of reincarnation.

-Q-

Qi (Chi)
The life-force that runs in our bodies. The cultivation of qi is a vital part Vajrayana practices. Examples of practices involving qi include, the Treasure Vase Breathing Practice, Tummo, the Nine Round Breaths Technique, and the Vajra Fist Exercise. When qi is developed and able to flow in the body, the channels and the five chakras can then be opened so that the entire body is filled with qi. Magnetic and spiritual energy develops as well as inner fire, which melts the drops at the brow point to descend, creating the sensation of Dharma Bliss. Grand Master uses qi to heal, transform offerings, empower items, among other things. Conversely, this energy can leak from the mind via craving, greed, anger, ignorance, and wrong views. To cultivate the mind is to cultivate qi, and to cultivate qi is to cultivate the mind.

-R-

Rainbow Temple
This retreat center that Grand Master Lu built in the Cascade Mountains in Western Washington State was known as the Rainbow Villa. As of 2008 it was declared a temple and is now called the "Rainbow Temple."

Raksasa
Evil and violent demons referred to as "man-eaters."

Reincarnation
In Buddhism, as in Hinduism and various other religions, it is believed that after one dies the spirit enters the bardo realm as it prepares for its next rebirth. One may be reborn in any of the six realms of samsara: hell, heaven, human, animal, asura or hungry ghost. It is also possible for an individual to reincarnate out of samsara and into a pure land, which provides an ideal environment for cultivation and meditation with the intent of reaching enlightenment. An accomplished or realized practitioner (by maintaining conscious awareness during the death process) can choose to return to samsara to continue benefiting sentient beings.

Relic (Sarira)
When a practitioner dies and is cremated, small pearl and jewel like objects are found in the remaining ashes which may multiply or radiate light.

Reverend Liaoming
Grand Master Lu met Reverend Liaoming (also known as Taoist Master Qingzhen) while he was residing on Jiji Mountain in Nantou County, Taiwan. Reverend Liaoming was a Vajrayana Master and the Fourteenth Generation Disciple of the Qingcheng Taoist School.

Ru-Wo Wo-Ru (Chinese, literally "Entering Me and I Enter")
Ru-wo, literally "entering me," is the Entering of the Principal Deity into Oneself. Wo-ru, literally "I enter," is the Release of Oneself into the Cosmic Consciousness. It is the merging of the self and the deity during the main essential practice of a sadhana, i.e., during samadhi. "Ru-wo Wo-ru Guan" is the Contemplation of Merging of the Self and the Deity during samadhi.

Sadhana (Sanskrit, literally "A Means of Accomplishing Something")
A means of accomplishment, a sequence of prescribed visualization, mudra, and mantra performed to cut through mental obscuration.

Sakya/Sakyapa/Flower Sect
This sect of Buddhism received the name Sakya, meaning "gray earth," due to the color of the ground where the first Sakya monastery was built in central Tibet. It is called the Flower Sect because a flower is the emblem of the family that runs the school. Originally founded by the famous scholar and translator Drokmi Lotsawa in the late eleventh century, it is primarily known for the *Lamdre*, or the "Path and Its Result," which is a system derived from the Hevajra Tantra and which provides a systematic teaching of the entire Buddhist path, including the Tripitaka (Vinaya, Sutra, and Abhidharma). This school is especially known for its eminence in scholarship and Tantric ritual.

Sakya Zhengkong
His Eminence Sakya Zhengkong Rinpoche transmitted the Sakya School's central teaching, Lamdre (The Fruit and its Path), and gave the Acharya Empowerment to Living Buddha Lian-sheng.

Sariras (Sanskrit, literally "Pearl-like")
When an accomplished practitioner dies and is cremated, small pearl and jewel-like objects (relics) are found in the remaining ashes which may multiply or radiate light.

Sastra
In Sanskrit, "treatise," a term used to refer to works contained in the various Buddhist canons attributed to various Indian masters. In this sense, the term is distinguished from SUTRA, a discourse regarded as the word of the Buddha or spoken with his sanction. In English, the word "commentary" is often rendered. In the Buddhist context, the

genre is typically a form of composition that explains the words or intention of the Buddha.

Sentient beings
Broadly speaking, all beings with awareness who have not attained enlightenment and become buddhas. More narrowly, all living beings with awareness within the six realms of reincarnation.

Shakyamuni Buddha
Siddhartha Gautama was born in Lumbini, India (modern day Nepal) sometime between 563 BCE to 483 BCE. He later became known as Shakyamuni Buddha. "Shakya" was his clan name and "muni" means great sage, thus, "the great sage of the Shakya clan." At the age of twenty-nine he left his home, and achieved enlightenment under the Bodhi Tree at age thirty-five. He became the founder of Buddhism and spread the dharma to all beings.
Shiva (The Destroyer)
One of the three primary deities of Hinduism. The other two deities are Vishnu (the preserver) and Brahma (the creator). The main iconographical attributes of Shiva are the third eye on his forehead, the serpent around his neck, the adorning crescent moon, the holy river Ganga flowing from his matted hair, the trishula as his weapon and the damaru. Shiva is also known as Mahesvara. See Mahesvara.

Siddhi (Sanskrit, literally "Accomplishment" or "Ability")
Refers to the accomplishments that come with spiritual practice. It may be the transcendental siddhi of attaining nirvana or it may refer to more mundane abilities like flying, clairvoyance, clairaudience, invisibility, everlasting youth, or powers of transmutation. The more esteemed accomplishments are: renunciation, compassion, unshakable faith, and the correct view.

Six Realms of Samsara
Comprised of the six realms: (1) devas (gods); (2) asuras; (3) humans; (4) animals; (5) hungry ghosts; (6) beings in hell. Sentient beings are stuck in the six realms until they attain enlightenment, thus freeing them of the need to be reborn in one of these realms.

Sixteenth Gyalwa Karmapa (August 14, 1924 – November 5, 1981)
Spiritual leader of the Karma Kagyu lineage of Tibetan Buddhism. The first incarnation of the Karmapa was in 1110 AD making this the longest line of Tibetan Tulkus. His Holiness the 16th Gyalwa Karmapa bestowed the highest empowerment of the Five-Buddha Crown Empowerment on Living Buddha Lian-sheng.

Sixth Patriarch Huineng (638 AD – 713 AD)
A Chinese Zen master who is one of the most important figures in the entire Chinese Buddhist tradition, he is said to have advocated an immediate and direct approach of Buddhist practice to attain enlightenment. In this regard, he is considered the founder of the "Sudden Enlightenment" Southern Zen School of Buddhism.

Skillful Means
Also translated as "expedient means" or "skill in means," "skillful means" is translation of the Sanskrit word upaya. The term, skillful means, refers to adjusting the teachings according to the capacities and the needs of the audience while applying perfect insight of emptiness and compassion to guide them toward enlightenment.

Sravaka (Solitary Hearer/Sound Hearer) (Sanskrit, literally "listener")
A disciple of the Buddha who "listened" to his teachings. In Mahayana, a Sravaka refers one who attains enlightenment as an arhat by following the basic (Hinayana) vehicle.

Surupakaya Tathagata
The appearance of Surupakaya Tathagata is similar to Amitabha Buddha. He wears a kasaya and sits in the lotus position upon a thousand-petaled lotus seat. He looks compassionately upon sentient beings. Both his palms face outward with all fingers straight up except that the right thumb and the right index finger form a circle.

Sutra
Meaning "a thread that keeps things together" in Sanskrit which is the metaphor for a set of rules and principles. In Buddhism, sutras are discourses given by Shakyamuni Buddha. Its usage has broadened to designate discourses by other buddhas such as the *Mahavairocana Sutra* or other highly regarded sacred Buddhist texts, such as the *Platform Sutra.*

Sutrayana
Also referred to as Sutra Buddhism and Exoteric Buddhism, Sutrayana is a branch of Buddhism that teaches the truths which the Buddha taught openly to the public. This terminology is used to distinguish teachings that were open to the public from esoteric teachings that were revealed to high capacity disciples in private. Vajrayana Schools see teachings of Sutrayana as a foundation of Buddhist cultivation and its practices as accumulating causes that leads to liberation. Only when the students have completed their training in Sutrayana may they commence learning the Tantric System.

-T-

Talisman
Metaphysical amulets infused with the power of the creator. They are drawn onto paper and then burned and eaten or carried by the person wishing to use the talisman's power. They may be used to help cure

illnesses, offer protection from danger, create harmony in life, etc.

Tantra
Refers to the teachings of Vajrayana. It is the spiritual truth which seeks through various mystical means to unite the individual consciousness with the universal consciousness.

Tao (Dao)
Literally, "The path to the truth." Tao or Dao is a Chinese concept signifying 'way,' 'path,' 'route,' or sometimes more loosely, 'doctrine' or 'principle.' Cosmologically, Tao signifies the primordial essence or fundamental nature of the Universe.

Taoism (Daoism)
Focuses on nature, the relationship between humanity and the cosmos, health and longevity, and wu wei (action through inaction), which is thought to produce harmony with the universe.

Tathagata (Sanskrit, literally "Thus Come One" or "Thus Gone One")
A synonym for Buddha. It refers to the primordially pure Buddha-nature which can neither be created anew nor ever destroyed. This nature can remain obscured indefinitely if not purified and developed. See also Ten titles of a Buddha.

Tathata (Sanskrit, literally "Suchness" or "Thusness")
As a central concept of Buddhism, it denotes the way things are in truth or actuality. Some synonyms for this concept include emptiness (sunyata), thusness (tattva), the limit of reality (bhuta-koti), true suchness (bhuta-tathata) or dharmata.

Tathagatagarbha Consciousness
The Thus Come One's Treasury (Tathagatagarbha) or the Alaya

Consciousness (alaya-vijnana). The *Lankavatara Sutra* states that the tathagatagarbha is identical to the alaya-vijnana, known prior to awakening as the storehouse-consciousness or eighth consciousness. The alaya-vijnana is supposed to contain the pure seed, or tathagatagarbha, from which awakening arises. The synthesis of the tathagatagarbha-doctrine and the alaya-vijnana doctrine is further developed in the *Awakening of Faith in the Mahayana.*

Ten Titles of a Buddha
These include: Tathagata, Arhat, Samyak-sambuddha, Vidyacarana-sampanna; Sugata; Lokavid; Anuttara; Purusa-damya-sarathi; Sasta deva-manusyanm; Buddha-lokanatha, or Bhagavan.

Three Saints of the Western Paradise
(Three Holy Sages of the Western Land of Ultimate Bliss)
Particular to practitioners of Pure Land Buddhism or Amitabha worship, Amitabha Buddha and the two bodhisattvas, Avalokitesvara on his right and Mahasthamaprapta on his left, appear and welcome the dying person, and guide them to the Pure Land.

Thubten Dargye
Vajra Acharya Thubten Dargye of the Gelug School gave the Highest Yoga Tantra empowerment to Living Buddha Lian-sheng, among many other empowerments.

Treasure Source Tara
Treasure Source Tara is one of the twenty one transformations of Green Tara. Like Green Tara, she is the most compassionate of all Bodhisattvas. Treasure Source Tara responds to the prayers of sentient beings and bestows treasures, money, and valuable material to them. She is the Buddha Mother of the Wealth Gods of the Five Directions. Vajrayana cultivators who practice the Treasure Source Tara sadhana

will eliminate the hindrances of poverty and receive blessings of great fortune.

Treasure-spouting Mongoose (Nakula)
Keeper of all the jewels, who spews up all these riches when pinched by the god of wealth.

Tsongkhapa (1357-1419)
The founder of the Gelug Sect of Tibetan Buddhism. He set up strict rules for the Gelug Sect which contrasted with the much looser rules of the other three sects of Tibetan Buddhism at that time.

Twelve Divine Generals of Medicine Buddha
The twelve great vows of Medicine Buddha manifested into twelve "Karma Guardian Deities," who are also known as the "Twelve Divine Generals of Medicine Buddha" or "Twelve Yaksa Generals of Medicine Buddha." They surround Medicine Buddha according to their twelve designated directions.

Twelve Links of Dependent Origination (Sanskrit: Pratityasamutpada)
The principle of dependent origination is the basis of the Buddhist worldview. The Buddha observed that all phenomena come into existence as the aggregate of many causes and conditions. Nothing comes into being independently of other factors, hence the name, dependent origination. In this doctrine, there is no need for a creator. Twelve Links are: Ignorance, motivational tendencies, consciousness, name and form, the six senses, sense impression, sensation, attachment, grasping, process of rebirth, birth, and old age and death. By reversing the fundamental ignorance skillfully, one can break out the cyclic existence and attain liberation.

-U-

UcchusmaA Vajra protector who manifested from the heart of Shakyamuni Buddha. He is also known as the Great Sovereign Divine King Buddha. Ucchusma is also respectfully known as the Buddha of the Esoteric Ones, Mighty Kings of Great Supernatural Power. The reason he is named Ucchusma is because of his ability to eradicate filth as he possesses strong yang energy. He removes illnesses, eradicates calamities, enables one to acquire people's love and respect, prevents accidents from happening, allows one to receive great luck and fortune, subjugates enemies, and dares evil demons and ghosts to invade. His primary vow is to eat up all unclean objects. Because Ucchusma is full of yang energy, one who succeeds in this dharma practice will not be afraid of any filthy contaminations.

Utpala Flower
Half-closed lotus flower, night lotus; in addition to purity, it represents the self-procreative and female principle. Nilotpala is the blue utpala.

-V-

Vaidurya
Refers to the gemstone. The color of the gemstone plays a great role in Tibetan medicine. Hence, Medicine Buddha is called be-du-rya hod-kyi rgyal-po, or "King of the Vaidurya Light." Medicine Buddha is often depicted with blue radiance.

Vajra (Sanskrit, literally "Diamond Scepter"; Dorje)
A common ritual object in Vajrayana Buddhist practices which represents a thunderbolt, or diamond, which in turn represents being indestructible. It can symbolize the male aspect of enlightenment (skillful means), whereas the vajra bell represents the feminine aspect of enlightenment (wisdom).

Vajra Master (Vajra Acharya; Sanskrit, literally "Diamond Teacher")
A master of Vajrayana teachings who has achieved accomplishment in esoteric practices and can guide trainees to overcome spiritual obstacles toward enlightenment. In True Buddha School, the Vajra Masters are identified with yellow collars on their lama robes.

Vajra Protector (Dharma Protector, Wrathful Protector)
Enlightened beings that take on wrathful forms. Their function is to protect Buddhist practitioners.

Vajra Scepter
The vajra scepter is the most important ritual object in Vajrayana Buddhism. It symbolizes the method of compassion that, in combination with wisdom (symbolized by the bell), accomplish the transformations necessary for a cultivator to attain enlightenment. Vajra literally means "diamond" or "thunderbolt," signifying the crystal-clear, indestructible power of compassion.

Vajrakilaya
A Buddhist dharma protector who can traverse spiritually and fly due to his divine wings. Vajrakilaya serves as the wrathful form of Vajrasattva, and is also known as Karma Heruka. Vajrakilaya's three bodies encompass Yamantaka, Hayagriva, and Vajrapani; hence, Vajrakilaya represents these three wrathful deities. Vajrakilaya is the manifestation of the vows of Samantabhadra Tathagata, therefore he is also the collective manifestation of the vows of all bodhisattvas and buddhas. Vajrakilaya is also one of Padmasambhava's spiritual manifestation bodies.

Vajravarahi (Dorje Pakmo)
The leader and the grand chief of dakinis. Vajravarahi is the root

dakini and the dharma companion of Living Buddha Lian-sheng. For practitioners cultivating qi, channels, and light drops, these practices all require Vajravarahi because she is the principal deity for cultivating the samadhi of inner fire. She is like radiant flames in one's navel chakra. One cannot accomplish the samadhi of inner fire without Vajravarahi.

Vajrayana Buddhism (Sanskrit, literally "Diamond Vehicle")
Also known as the Vehicle of Indestructible Reality and Secret Mantrayana ("Mantra Vehicle"), is a form of Mahayana Buddhism in which the guru teaches an accelerated path to enlightenment through the practices of the three secrets of speech (chanting mantras), body (forming mudras), and mind (visualization). There is a vital element of the teacher-student relationship. The respect of the teacher is extremely vital in Vajrayana because the teacher is the living embodiment of the Three Jewels of the Buddha, Dharma, and Sangha.

Vishnu (The Preserver)
One of the three primary deities of Hinduism. The other two deities are Brahma (the creator) and Shiva (the destroyer). Vishnu is the preserver and protector of the universe. To preserve the universe, Vishnu returns to the earth in many forms of his avatara.

-W-

Water Repentance
A repentance ritual initiated by the monk Wu Da, based on the repentance of the holy Sangha.

Western Paradise (Western Paradise of Ultimate Bliss, Western Pure Land: Sukhavati in Sanskrit, literally "Land of Bliss")
The Pure Land of Amitabha Buddha. A pure land is a place where

many Buddhists aspire to be reborn, where they may cultivate diligently until reaching enlightenment, without fear of falling back into the six realms of reincarnation. It is a realm of consciousness rather than an actual locality.

White Skeleton Visualization
A method taught by Shakyamuni Buddha to get rid of improper thoughts. The sexual object is contemplated as transforming into a heap of white bones so as to lose attraction to it.

White Tara
Her two eyes together with one ajna eye, one eye in each palm and sole of each foot make seven eyes. Therefore, she is also known as "Seven-eyed Buddha Mother." "White Tara" is a sad teardrop emanation of Avalokitesvara. She is also one of the twenty-one emanations of Tara. Her other alias is "Life Prolonging Rescuing Buddha Mother." "White Tara" is one of the Buddhist deities that treat sickness and prolong lives. Her body in white symbolizes "ceasing calamities." The third eye located in the center of her eyebrows can tell the cause of all epidemics and illnesses. Because of it, she can terminate them.

Wrathful Protector (Vajra Protector; Dharma Protector; Dharmapala)
An enlightened being that takes on a wrathful form and whose function is to protect Buddhist practitioners.

-X-

-Y-

Yaksa
A demon similar to a raksasa and is usually evil and violent. Some are benevolent, like in the case of the twelve yaksas who serve and protect

the Medicine Buddha. They aid and protect those who cultivate the Medicine Buddha Yoga. These twelve yaksas represent the twelve vows of the Medicine Buddha.

Yoga (Sanskrit, literally "Union")
In Buddhism, it is a method uniting an individual self with the Buddha. It includes physical and mental exercises which help one reach enlightenment.

Yoga Tantra (Yogatantra)
In Sanskrit, "Yogatantra." It is the third of four levels of tantra principally emphasizing internal action or yoga. It is ranked above Action Tantra (Kriyatantra) and Conduct or Performance Tantra (Caryatantra), but below Highest Yoga Tantra (Anuttarayogatantra).

Yogacara School (Sanskrit, literally "Practice of Yoga")
One of the major schools of Mahayana Buddhism, it is commonly called the Cittamatra (Mind Only) School as well as Vijnanavada (Way of Consciousness) and Vijnana-matra (Consciousness Only). Established by two brothers, Asanga and Vasubandhu, it was said that Asanga beseeched Maitreya Bodhisattva to reveal to him the true meaning of emptiness. In response, Maitreya Bodhisattva appeared to Asanga for five months explaining to him the meaning of emptiness which Asanga recorded down as the *Five Treatises of Maitreya*, which became the foundation of Yogacara philosophies.

The Yogacara School systematically analyzes cognition, consciousness and perceptions to overcome the ignorance that prevents one from breaking out of cyclic existence. It focuses on studying consciousness because it is the cause of cyclic existence. The eight consciousnesses defined by Yogacara are: (1) eye-consciousness; (2) ear-consciousness; (3) nose-consciousness; (4) tongue-consciousness; (5) body-consciousness; (6) thought-consciousness; (7) manas-consciousness; (8) alaya-consciousness.

Yogacara Ulka-mukha
The Ritual for Feeding of Hungry Ghosts or the Yoga Flaming Mouth Ceremony. "Ulka-mukha" (flaming mouth) is represented in the Buddhist sutras as a hungry ghost (preta). In addition to a very thin appearance, it has a throat that is no bigger than needles, and a mouth that spits out flame.

Yogic Response (Yogic Union)
By practicing mudras, mantras and visualizations the respective deity invoked and the practitioner is at an equal level with the Three Secrets (body, speech, and mind) of the Tathagata, and thus possesses limitless meritorious functions. Once the practitioner merges with the principal deity, he or she gains access into the dharma realm through this single gateway.

-Z-

Also From US Daden Culture

Sheng-yen Lu Book Collection 158:
Contemplation Under the Lonesome Light

Sale Price: $12.00 USD
ISBN: 978-0-9960699-9-1

Sheng-yen Lu Book Collection 163:
Crossing the Ocean of Life and Death

Sale Price: $12.00 USD
ISBN: 978-0-9841561-0-0

Sheng-yen Lu Book Collection 166:
Travel to Worlds Beyond
Sale Price: $12.00 USD

ISBN: 978-0-9841561-2-2

Sheng-yen Lu Book Collection 200:
Pages and Pages of Enlightenment
Sale Price: $12.00 USD
ISBN: 978-0-9841561-5-3

3440 Foothill Blvd. • Oakland, CA 94601 • U.S.A. • www.usdaden.com

Also From US Daden Culture

Sheng-yen Lu Book Collection 202:
Sightings from Thousands of Miles Away

Sale Price: $12.00 USD
ISBN: 978-0-9841561-3-9

Sheng-yen Lu Book Collection 204:
The Divine Book

Sale Price: $12.00 USD
ISBN: 978-0-9960699-0-8

Sheng-yen Lu Book Collection 218:
Remembrance of the Moon River

Sale Price: $12.00 USD
ISBN: 978-0-9858080-6-8

Sheng-yen Lu Book Collection 220:
Q&A with A Contemporary Dharma King, Vol. 2

Sale Price: $12.00 USD
ISBN: 978-0-9963807-2-0

3440 Foothill Blvd. • Oakland, CA 94601 • U.S.A. • www.usdaden.c